WOOD DALE PUBLIC LIBRARY
3 1687 00178 2249

D1517320

FEB 2 6 2002

DISCARD
WOOD DALE DISTRICT LIBRARY
WOOD DALE, ILLINOIS

TOP DOT
Tales

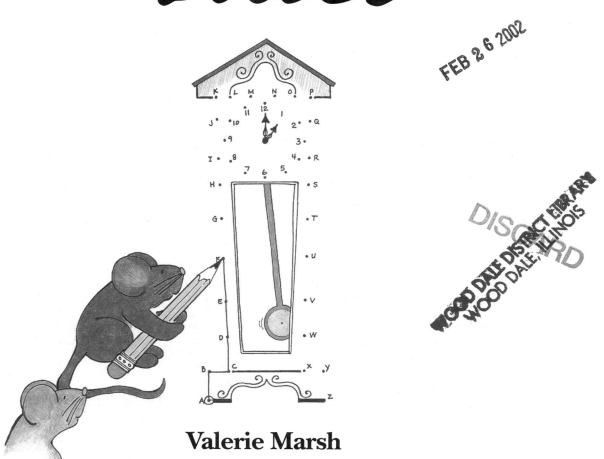

Valerie Marsh
Illustrated by Patrick Luzadder

Alleyside Press®

Fort Atkinson, Wisconsin

To all teachers, media specialists, parents and other adults who have found great pleasure and satisfaction in connecting with children through the power of storytelling.

Published by Alleyside Press, an imprint of Highsmith Press
Highsmith Press
W5527 Highway 106
P.O. Box 800
Fort Atkinson, Wisconsin 53538-0800
1-800-558-2110
hpress@highsmith.com
www.hpress.highsmith.com

© Valerie Marsh, 2001
Cover design: Debra Neu Sletten

The paper used in this publication meets the minimum requirements of American National Standard for Information Science — Permanence of Paper for Printed Library Material. ANSI/NISO Z39.48-1992.

All rights reserved. Printed in the United States of America.
The purchase of this book entitles the individual librarian or teacher to reproduce copies for use in the library or classroom. The reproduction of any part for an entire school system or for commercial use is strictly prohibited. No form of this work may be reproduced or transmitted or recorded without written permission from the publisher.

Library of Congress Cataloging-in-Publication Data
Marsh, Valerie
    Top dot tales / by Valerie Marsh ; illustrated by Patrick K. Luzadder.
        p. cm.
    ISBN 1-57950-004-8 (alk. paper)
        1. Storytelling. 2. Early childhood education–Activity programs. 3.
Creative activities and seat work. I. Title.
    LB1042 .M28745 2000
    372.13–dc21   2001001818
                                                                CIP

Contents

Introduction   5

Nursery Rhymes

 1. Baa, Baa, Black Sheep   7

 2. Hey, Diddle, Diddle   9

 3. Hickory, Dickory, Dock   11

 4. Humpty Dumpty   13

 5. Itsy Bitsy Spider   15
    Challenge Activity—Draw a Spider Web

 6. Jack and Jill   19

 7. Little Miss Muffet   21
    Challenge Activity—Draw a Spider Web

 8. Old Mother Hubbard   23

 9. This Little Piggy   25
    Challenge Activity—Draw a Pig

 10. Twinkle, Twinkle, Little Star   29

Songs, Tales, and Poems

 11. The Ants Go Marching   31
    Supplement Poster

 12. Down by the Bay   36

 13. The Farmer in the Dell   38

 14. Fuzzy Wuzzy   40
    Challenge—Bear Maze

 15. Coyote and the Marshmallows   43
    Challenge Activity—Coyote Maze

16. Frog's Trick   47

17. The Lion and the Mouse   49

18. Three Silly Wishes   52

19. Five Little Monkeys and Mr. Alligator   56

20. Rabbit and Snake   59

Celebrations

21. Birthday Presents   62

22. Valentine Wishes   65

23. St. Patrick's Day   67

24. Spring Rainbows   70

25. Earth Day   72

26. The School Bus *(First Day of School)*   75

27. Halloween   78

28. An Alphabet Turkey *(Thanksgiving)*   *81*

29. Crayons for the Holidays   84
(Christmas, Kwanzaa, or Hanukkah)

Seasons

30. Fall Leaves   87

31. Winter Snowman   89

32. Spring Butterfly   92

33. Summer Sailboat   95

Introduction

We all love a good story! And as we listen to a story, we use many skills to make sense of it and integrate it into our lives. Listening to and participating in the stories included in this book provides children opportunities for practicing listening and comprehension skills, including:

- Using their imagination to create mental pictures of the tale;

- Developing their oral communication skills by hearing new words, phrases, and ideas;

- Refining auditory discrimination skills;

- Strengthening critical thinking skills;

- Improving their creative abilities;

- Expanding their active listening abilities;

- Growing their love for books and reading.

Use this book to help your children with these pre-reading and pre-math skills:

- Patterning with two or three objects;

- Reading and writing left to right;

- Reading and writing top to bottom;

- Recognizing letters of the alphabet;

- Matching capital and lower case letters;

- Recognizing numerals 1–100;

- Counting by ones, twos, fives, and tens;

- Sequencing skills;

- One-to-one correspondence skills;

- Drawing skills;

- Literature appreciation;

- Listening skills;

- Following direction skills;

- Fine motor skills;

- Visual discrimination.

Stories are powerful. When we see the rapt expression on a listening child's face or hear the unplanned sigh or laughter from listeners at a particularly funny or sad part of the story, we are witnessing the mysterious, magical, and timeless power of storytelling. Yes, stories have great power. "Connect" your children up to one today!

How to Use this Book

Select the story you like, and photocopy the picture for the children. Give each child the picture, then share the story with them. Recite or sing the nursery rhyme or folk song together. After everyone is very familiar with it, then let them connect the dots.

Many stories involve children by asking them to connect the dots as you tell the story. All you need to do is provide a copy of the picture and crayons or markers for each child.

Additional activities are provided at the end of each story. Some stories have additional activities to extend the story's enjoyment.

Storytelling Rules

1. There are *no* rules.

2. Tell stories from this book that you like.

3. Keep it simple.

4. Relax and storyteach the story—don't perform it.

5. Encourage the children to tell these stories.

6. Children are listening for your story—not your mistakes!

7. Retell, retell, retell!

8. Enjoy!

Additional Activities

1. Give each child a strip of small dot stickers. Let them stick the dots on their paper wherever they choose. Then encourage them to connect up the dots with a crayon or marker. For a partner activity, let one child place the dots on the paper and the friend connect them. For a challenge activity, have the children number their dots one to ten as they stick the dots on their paper. Then the partner can connect the dots with a crayon.

2. Show older children how they can make their own dot-to-dot on the computer using a drawing program.

3. Use cotton swabs to paint dots inside a simple outline of an animal such as a dog. Connect the dots when the paint is dry.

4. If you celebrate One Hundred Day at your school, have children draw a simple outline of an object or animal. Have children make a dot-to-dot up to 100.

5. Use an ink pad and your thumb to make your own dots for an original dot-to-dot.

6. Bingo markers (tubes of paint with a sponge applicators) make great dots. Children can draw their own picture, or they can use a pre-drawn picture and add their own dots.

Baa, Baa, Black Sheep

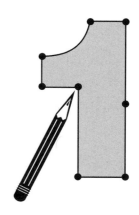

Refrain:

Baa, baa, black sheep,
Have you any wool?
(Start at the big star and connect dots 1 to 15.)

Yes, sir, yes, sir,
Three bags full;
(Start with the circle dot and connect uppercase A to lowercase a through G to g.)

One for the master,
(Connect dots H to h through N to n.)

One for the dame,
(Now connect T to t through O to o.)

And one for the little boy
Who lives down the lane.
(Finally, connect the dots U to u through Z to z.)

(Refrain)

Activities

1. Finish and discuss the picture. After the children have connected the upper case letters of the alphabet to the lower case letters, ask them to count how many bags of wool they drew. Compare the number of bags in the poem to the number of bags in your picture. Do you draw more or less bags? Which bag is the biggest? Which bag is the smallest?

2. Make sheep. After the children have connected the dots to make their picture, let them glue cotton balls onto their sheep. Show them how to stretch and fluff up the cotton balls before gluing onto their paper.

3. Learn more about sheep. Discuss the process of how we get wool from the sheep to make wool fabric. Show the children an item of wool clothing. Point out any wool items that you or the children might be wearing.

4. Using picture books or posters, recite or sing other nursery rhymes with the children. Use nursery rhymes to discuss rhyming words. Ask the children to identify the pair of rhyming words in this poem. Point out that other nursery rhymes have more sets of words that rhyme than this one does.

Name

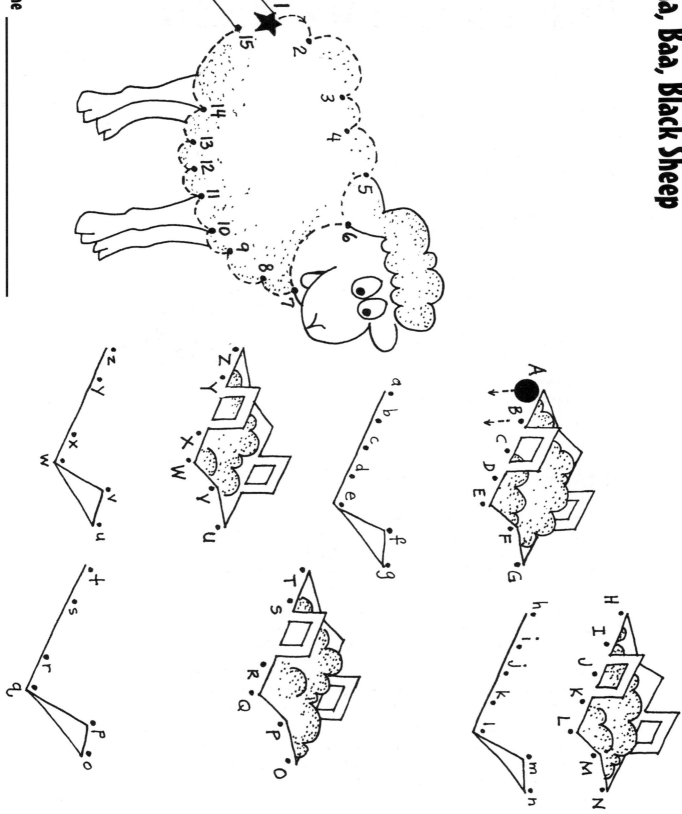

From *Top Dot Tales*. Copyright © 2001 by Valerie Marsh (Alleyside Press)

Hey, Diddle, Diddle

Hey, diddle, diddle,

The cat and the fiddle,
(Starting with the star, connect the dots 1 to 9 for the cat's face.)

The cow jumped over the moon;
(Starting with the circle, connect the dots A through M to draw the moon.)

The little dog laughed to see such sport,
(Starting with the triangle, connect the dots 1 to 6 to make the dog's ears.)

And the dish ran away with the spoon.
(Starting with the square, connect the dots N to Z to make the dish.)

Activities

1. Retell the poem. Recite or sing the poem again, and add the appropriate animal noises. Children may wish to color the picture.

2. Make puppets. Have a puppet show with these characters! Draw a circle around the cat, the moon, the dog, and the dish. Children may cut out or color one or more of these objects. After stapling them to a popsicle stick, use the puppets to recite this nursery rhyme.

3. Learn about the moon. Help children trace around a small, unripened banana to make a moon. Discuss the similarities between the two shapes. Show pictures of the moon in other phases.

4. Review shapes. Discuss the shapes that the children made. Ask them to identify the shape of the cat's face (circle), the dog's ears (triangle) and the dish (oval). Provide a snack of circle, oval, triangle, and square crackers.

Hey, Diddle, Diddle

Name _____

From *Top Dot Tales*. Copyright © 2001 by Valerie Marsh (Alleyside Press)

Hickory, Dickory, Dock

Hickory, dickory, dock,
(Find the star on the mouse. Draw from 1 around to 12.)

The mouse ran up the clock.
(Start at the circle and draw from A to K.)

The clock struck one,
(Draw from K to P.)

The mouse ran down,
(Draw down the other side of the clock from P to Z.

Hickory, dickory, dock.

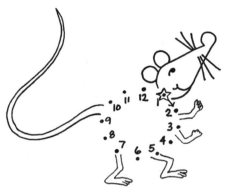

Activities

1. Finish the drawing. Let the children draw the circle of the clock face (numbers 1–12). Discuss the similarities between the clock and mouse drawing. (The clock face and mouse body are both round. They both have the same numbers on them.) Children may wish to color their picture.

2. Read mice books, both fiction and nonfiction.

3. Make a mouse nest. Gather up scraps of paper and cloth, packing peanuts, bubble wrap, and shredded paper. Encourage children to first draw a mouse on their paper and then make a nest for their mouse by gluing these materials around their mouse.

4. Do fingerprint mice. Show children how to use an ink pad to make a finger or thumb print on their paper. They can then use a felt tip marker to make whiskers for their mice, legs, tail, etc. for their mice.

Hickory, Dickory, Dock

Name _____

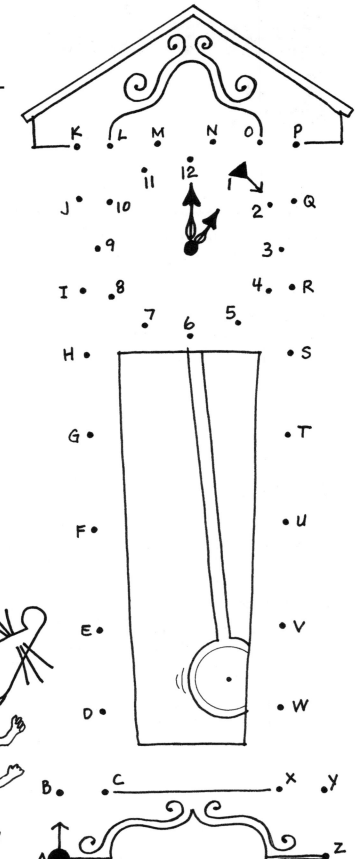

From *Top Dot Tales*. Copyright © 2001 by Valerie Marsh (Alleyside Press)

Humpty Dumpty

Humpty Dumpty sat on the wall,

Humpty Dumpty had a great fall;

All the King's horses

And all the King's men

Couldn't put Humpty together again.

Activities

1. Draw Humpty Dumpty's wall. Trace the dashed line A to M, a to m, N to Z, n to z. Draw lines between the upper- and lowercase letters to make the bricks on the wall.

2. Match upper- and lowercase letters. Write several uppercase letters in a line on the chalkboard or dry marker board. Then, write a line of lowercase letters next to it. Let the children match up the letters. Encourage the children to write their own sets of upper- and lowercase letters.

3. Make Humpty Dumpty and his wall. Glue small pieces of egg shells (rinsed and dried) onto a piece of paper in the shape of Humpty Dumpty. Dab a small, rectangular sponge in red paint and sponge paint several lines of rectangles for Humpty's wall.

4. Practice counting. Count how many bricks on Humpty Dumpty's wall. How many on the top row? How many on the bottom row? How many in the middle row?

Humpty Dumpty

Name _____

A B C D E F G H I J K L M

a b c d e f g h i j k l m

N O P Q R S T U V W X Y Z

n o p q r s t u v w x y z

From *Top Dot Tales*. Copyright © 2001 by Valerie Marsh (Alleyside Press)

Itsy Bitsy Spider

Recite or sing the poem several times together before doing this activity.

The itsy bitsy spider
went up the water spout.
(Start on the star and draw up the water spout. Follow the numbers 1 to 10.)

Down came the rain
and washed the spider out.
(Start on the circle and connect the letters A to Z to make the water spout.)

Out came the sun
and dried up all the rain.
(Start on the square and connect the dots by tens, 0–100, to make the sun.)

And the itsy bitsy spider
went up the spout again.
(Start on the triangle and connect the dots by tens to make the spider, 10–100.)

Activities

1. Learn opposites. This poem is a great way to start a discussion about opposites. Ask the children to name some opposites in the poem. (Sun, rain. Wet, dry. Up, down. Happy, sad.) Name other opposite words and write them on the chalkboard or chart paper. Ask for a volunteer to act out a pair of opposites. Encourage children to guess what their friend is acting out.

2. Spider on the waterspout project. Give children a paper rectangle to glue onto their paper to make a house. Or have them draw a house onto their paper. Then put a spider ring on a plastic drinking straw and tape the straw at both ends to the side of the child's house. The child can slide her spider up and down the "water-spout" as she recites "The Itsy Bitsy Spider" poem.

3. Paper plate spider web: Cut one inch slits around the edges of small black paper plates. Give each child a length of white yarn. Secure one end of the yarn to the back of the plate with masking tape. Show the children how to wrap the yarn around the plate by sliding it into the slits. The yarn criss-crossing over itself makes a nice web effect. Children may use as much or as little yarn as they want. When finished, secure other end of the yarn to the back with tape. For the final touch, tie a small plastic spider to the yarn, or put a spider sticker on the plate.

4. Spider Ring Relay: Divide the class into two or more teams. For each team, put five spider rings in a bucket. The first child on each team puts on all five rings and runs down to designated spot and back. She then takes off all the rings and gives them to the next person in line. This person puts the rings on, runs down and back and gives the rings to the next person. The team to finish first, wins! Note: To make this relay easier or faster, use just one or two rings.

5. Challenge activity: Draw a spider web (see worksheet on page 18).

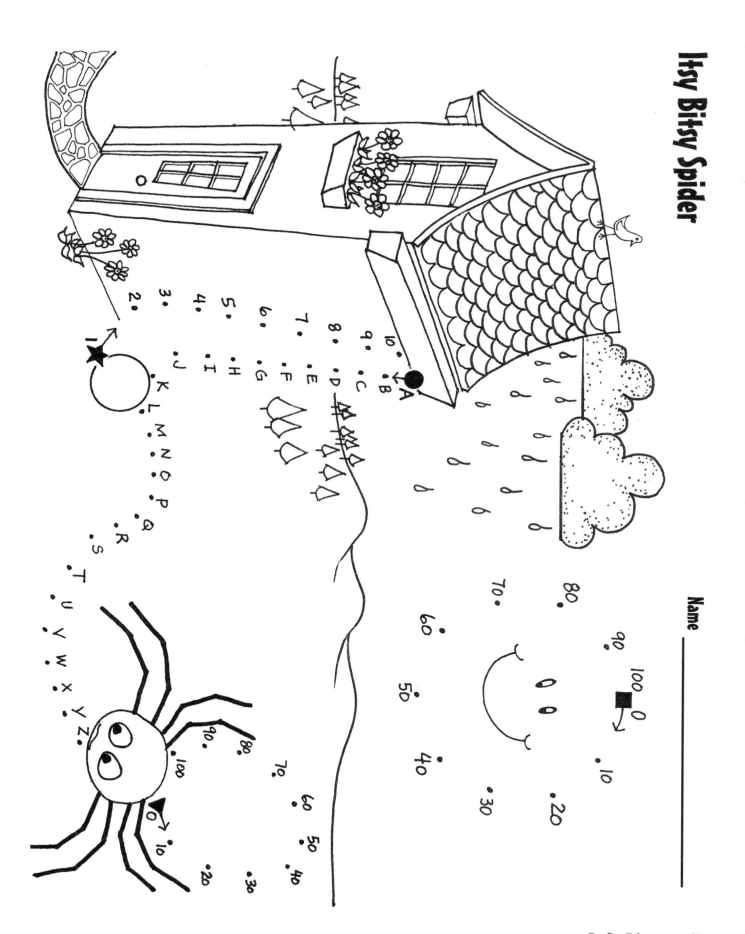

Itsy Bitsy Spider

Name _____

Draw a Spider Web

Name _____

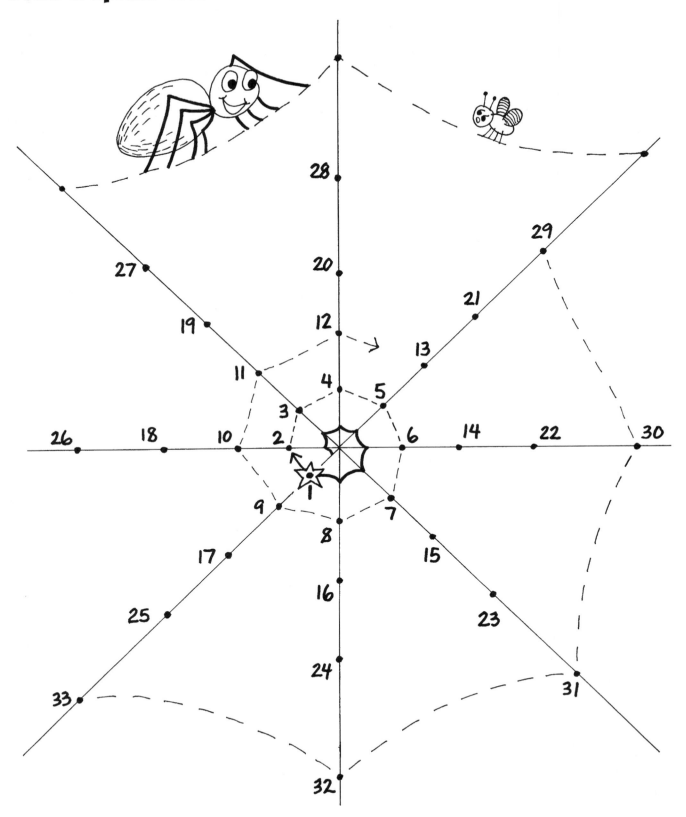

From *Top Dot Tales*. Copyright © 2001 by Valerie Marsh (Alleyside Press)

Jack and Jill

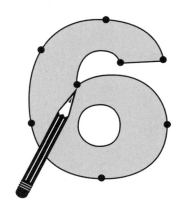

Jack and Jill
went up the hill,
to fetch a pail of water.
(Notice the stars, squares, triangles and circles. Let's draw Jack going up the hill. Start at the big star and connect the circles and stars with your crayon or pencil. Notice that this makes a pattern—circle, star, circle, star. Draw all the way up the hill. Stop your line when you get to the well. Then draw Jill going up the hill. Start at the smaller star.)

Jack fell down,
and broke his crown,
and Jill came tumbling after.
(Now let's start at the well and draw our lines down the hill. Connect the square, triangle, square, triangle, square, triangle all the way down the hill.)

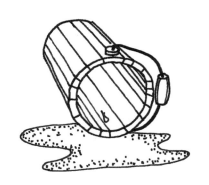

Activities

1. Recite the poem together again. Let the children retrace their lines up and down the hill. This is also good for left to right practice. Let them draw Jack and Jill in their picture, either climbing up or falling down.

2. Discuss word meanings. Reviewing the meaning of the word "crown" would be helpful for many children. Discuss why the poem uses the word "crown" and not head. Help them find the other pair of rhyming words.

3. Learn rhyming words. Continue with rhyming words by naming other words that rhyme with down—"brown," "frown," "town," "clown." Name words that rhyme with Jill—"will," "fill," "still," "drill," "grill."

4. Practice on patterns. Focus on the pattern the children followed as they drew their lines up the hill and back down the hill. Have the children make their own patterns with two differently shaped blocks, crayon colors, stringing beads, or other manipulatives available in the classroom. Children may then color their pattern on paper. Large grid graph paper works very well for young children.

Jack and Jill

From *Top Dot Tales*. Copyright © 2001 by Valerie Marsh (Alleyside Press)

Little Miss Muffet

Recite this nursery rhyme several times with the children so that everyone feels comfortable with it before doing this activity.

Little Miss Muffet
(Start at star. Draw from 1 to 2 to 3 to 4 to 5.)

Sat on a tuffet,
(Start at circle. Draw from 1 to 5.)

Eating her curds and whey;
(Start at triangle. Draw 1 to 5.)

There came a big spider,
Who sat down beside her
(Start at square. Draw from 1 to 5.)

And frightened Miss Muffet away.
(Draw the spider's drop line, 6 to 7.)

What letter do the legs of the spider make? (The letter M.) What words in the story start with the letter M? (Miss, Muffet) Can you think of any other words that start with the letter M?

Activities

1. Learn about spiders. How many legs does a spider have? How many body parts? Share some nonfiction spider books with the children.

2. Make a spider to eat. (Always check for food allergies.) Let each child spread peanut butter or ready-made icing on a circular cracker. After he counts out eight pretzel sticks, help him put four on each side of the cracker for the legs. Put a second cracker on top if desired. Using a dab of peanut butter, stick red hots or raisins on the top cracker for the eyes. Any round food such as dough-nut holes, rice cakes, bagels could also be used for the spider body. Styrofoam balls cut in half and toothpicks can also be used to make a spider if non-food items are to be used.

3. Make a spider headband. Cut a two inch wide length of black or brown paper for the headband. Cut one inch wide by nine inches long strips of paper. Let each child count out eight spider legs and glue onto her headband. (Legs should hang down when the child wears the headband. Legs may be fan folded for added effect.) Children may wish to add eyes to their spider to the front of their spider headband.

4. Challenge activity: Draw a spider web (see Itsy Bitsy Spider worksheet on page 18).

Little Miss Muffet

Name _____

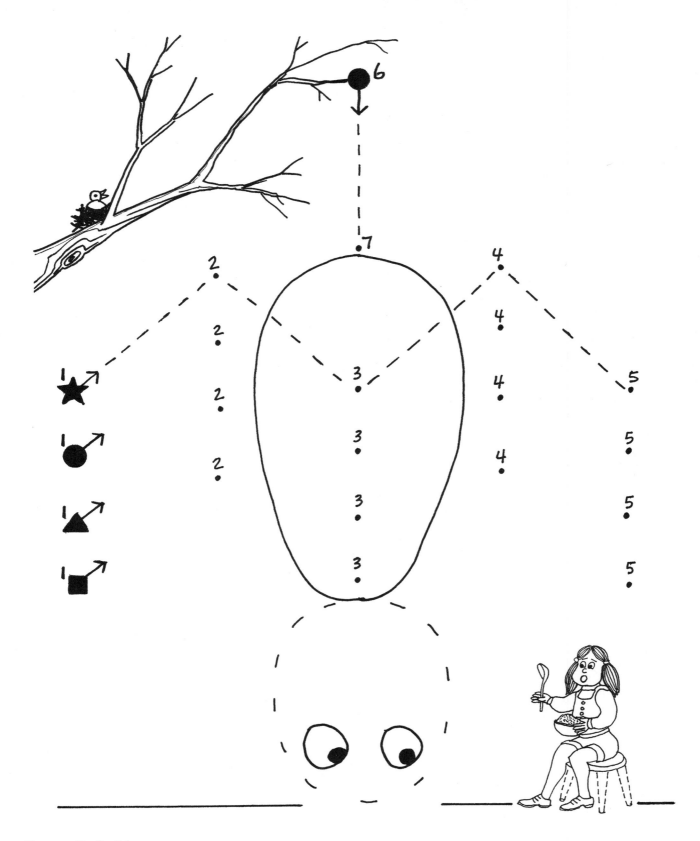

From *Top Dot Tales.* Copyright © 2001 by Valerie Marsh (Alleyside Press)

Old Mother Hubbard

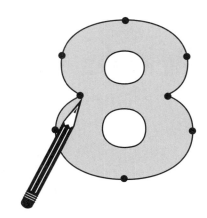

Old Mother Hubbard
(Draw from D to d.)

Went to the cupboard,
(Draw from O to o.)

To fetch her poor dog a bone;
(Draw from G to g.)

But when she got there
(Draw from B to b.)

The cupboard was bare
(Draw from O to o.)

And so the poor dog had none.
(Draw from N to n.)

Starting at the circle, trace the bone for the dog.
Connect all the dots from 1 to 15.

Activities

1. Recite the poem again together. Let the children color the dog, cupboard, and bone if time permits.

2. Left to Right activities: Point out that they drew all the lines (shelves) on the cupboard from left to right. Have the children trace over these lines again with their fingers. Encourage them to pay attention to the left to right motion of their finger.

3. Math activities: Provide additional left to right activities by counting the days of the month on the calendar, using a counting chart, and using a teaching chart.

4. Enrichment: Point out that the letters down the side of the cupboard spell "dog bone." Give each child a real dog treat. (Inexpensive and available at grocery stores.) Caution the children not to eat it! Let them glue the real dog bone onto the bone picture that the children traced.

Old Mother Hubbard

Name _____

D O G B O N E

d o g b o n e

13

12

14

15   1

2

3

4

11   9   8   7

5

10   6

    From *Top Dot Tales*. Copyright © 2001 by Valerie Marsh (Alleyside Press)

This Little Piggy

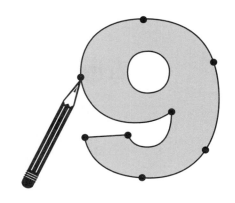

Recite this poem together before doing the drawing activity.

This little piggy went to market,

This first little pig had to walk all the way around his block to get there. *(Start at the big star. Draw a circle all the way around to number 9. This is the pig's head.)* He took some money with him so he could buy something nice. *(Draw a small circle around each dot for eyes.)*

This little piggy stayed home,

The second little pig lived in a circle house. *(Start at the circle. Draw a large circle from number 10 all the way around to 18. This is the pig's body.)* Smoke came out of his chimney. *(Trace over the dotted line for tail.)*

This little piggy had roast beef,

Roast beef was really not this third little pig's favorite food. Pizza was. So he cut his roast beef into triangles and pretended he was eating pizza. He ate two pieces. Let's draw the third little pig's pizza. *(Connect up the three little triangles into a bigger triangle for each ear.)*

This little piggy had none,

The fourth little pig looked in all of his cupboards but he could not find any food. Do you know what this little pig's cupboards really were? They were really shoeboxes. Let's draw the fourth little pigs empty food cupboards. *(Trace over dashed lines: a to b to c to d for the first shoebox cupboard. Trace from e to f to g to h for the second shoebox cupboard. Trace from i to j to k to l for the third shoebox cupboard. Trace from m to n to o to p for the last shoebox cupboard. These are the pig's four legs.)*

This little piggy cried "wee, wee, wee" all the way home.

Why do you think he said "Wee, wee?" Was he laughing or crying? Look at the pig that you drew. Isn't he great?

Activities

1. Finish drawing the pig. What is your pig missing? Yes, he is missing a mouth. Can you draw a big smile for your pig?

2. Review shapes. Point out the shapes of triangle, rectangle and circle. How many circles does your pig have? Rectangles? Triangles?

3. Make a paper plate pig. Let children color a pig face on a small paper plate. Glue or staple the small plate to a larger paper plate. Glue on construction paper feet. Attach a pipe cleaner tail. (You can make it curly by twisting it around a pencil first.)

4. Make a pig snack. Using plastic knives, help children spread pink icing on a popcorn or rice cake. Use banana slices, raisins, or small candies for the eyes and nose. Use string licorice or a green pepper slice for the pig's mouth.

5. Challenge activity: Draw a pig! (See worksheet on page 28.)

This Little Piggy

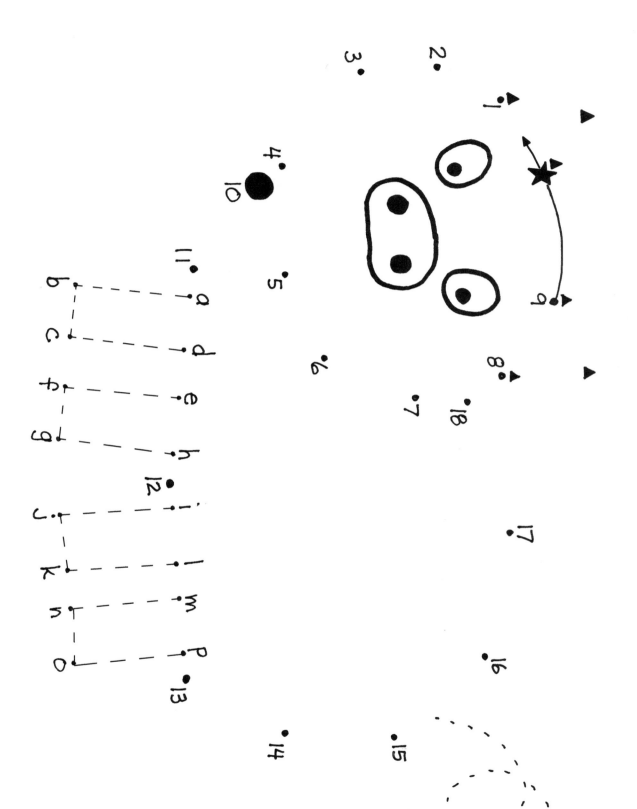

Name _____

Draw a Pig

Name _____

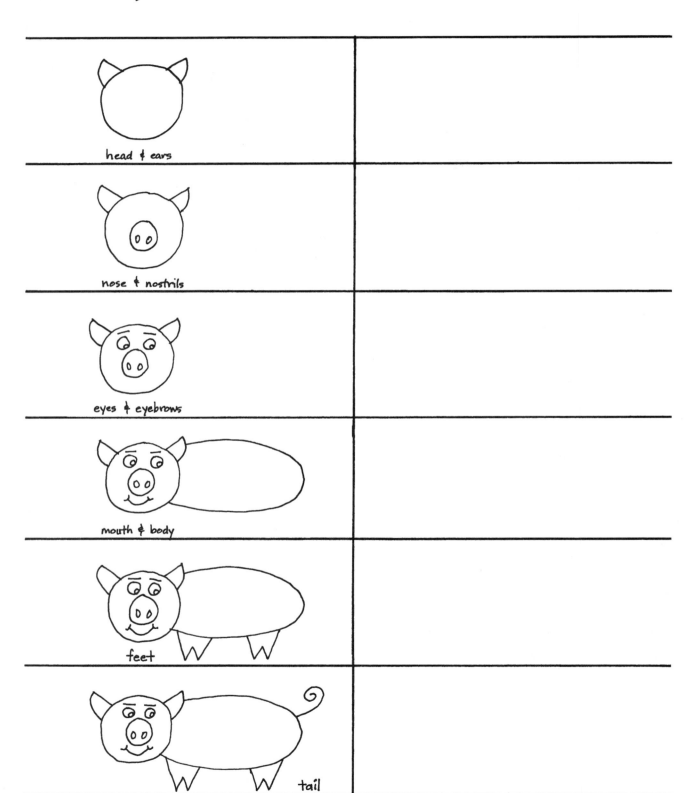

head & ears

nose & nostrils

eyes & eyebrows

mouth & body

feet

tail

   From *Top Dot Tales*. Copyright © 2001 by Valerie Marsh (Alleyside Press)

Twinkle, Twinkle, Little Star

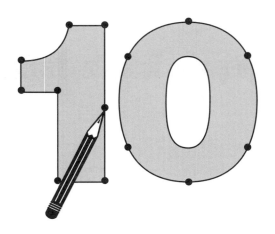

Verse 1:

Twinkle, twinkle, little star,
How I wonder what you are!
Up above the world so high,
Like a diamond in the sky.
Twinkle, twinkle, little star,
How I wonder what you are.

Verse 2:

Draw with me. I'll draw with you.
Use your pencil, paper too!
Connect the dots, 1, 2, 3,
Then the letters, A, B, C.
Now you drew a star with me,
Twinkle, twinkle, little star.

Activities

1. Draw the star using the two patterns on page 30. Choose the type you like best and photocopy that star only. Four stars will fit on one page. Depending on the age of the child, you might want to let them use their fingers to connect the dots first. When everyone is comfortable with the 1, 2, 3 and A, B, C sequence, give each child a crayon or marker. First, sing the familiar verse of "Twinkle" and then sing the new verse. Sing the song slowly enough that everyone can draw it together. Children can then draw more stars on recycled paper.

2. Make a mural. Once they get the hang of it, children love to draw stars. Capitalize on this interest by making a classroom "star" mural. On blue or other colored paper, let children draw stars with a variety of colored markers.

3. Use sign language. Sing the song together as a class. Using the illustrations below, show the children the signs for "star," "world," and "sky" then sing the song again using the signs.

Star 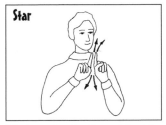	**World** 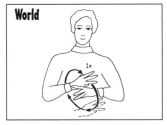	**Sky** 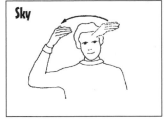
"1"-shape hands. Alternately strike index fingers against each other.	"W"-shape hands. Circle RH "W" forward then under LH "W."	Arc flat RH from left to right over head.

Twinkle, Twinkle, Little Star

Name _____

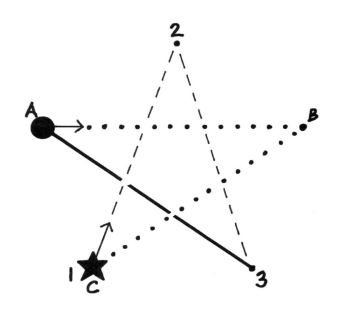

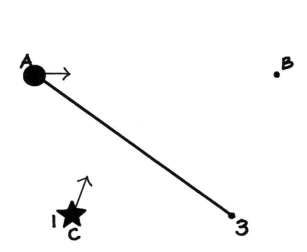

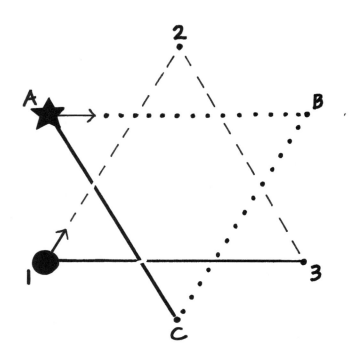

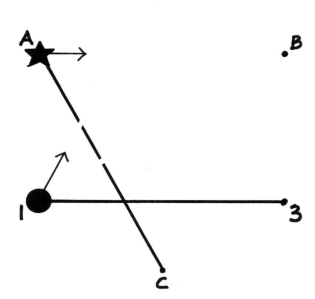

From *Top Dot Tales.* Copyright © 2001 by Valerie Marsh (Alleyside Press)

The Ants Go Marching

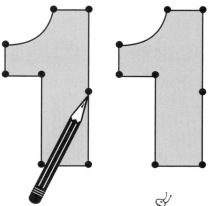

Sing to the tune of "When Johnny Comes Marching Home."

The ants go marching 1 by 1, hur-rah, hurrah.
The ants go marching 1 by 1, hur-rah, hurrah.
The ants go marching 1 by 1,
the little one stopped to *(choose one)*:
    suck his thumb; play his drum.
And they all go marching down
to the ground, to get out of the rain.
Boom, Boom, Boom,
Boom, Boom, Boom, Boom.

The ants go marching 2 by 2, hur-rah, hurrah.
The ants go marching 2 by 2, hur-rah, hurrah.
The ants go marching 2 by 2, the lit-tle one stopped to *(choose one)*:
    tie his shoe; cry boo-hoo.
And they all go marching down
to the ground, to get out of the rain.
Boom, Boom, Boom,
Boom, Boom, Boom, Boom.

The ants go marching 3 by 3, hurrah, hurrah.
The ants go marching 3 by 3, hurrah, hurrah.
The ants go marching 3 by 3, the lit-tle one stopped to *(choose one)*:
    climb a tree; scratch his knee.
And they all go marching down
to the ground, to get out of the rain.
Boom, Boom, Boom,
Boom, Boom, Boom, Boom.

The ants go marching 4 by 4,
hurrah, hurrah.

The ants go marching 4 by 4, hur-rah, hurrah.
The ants go marching 4 by 4 the lit-tle one stopped to *(choose one)*:
    wash the floor; shut the door.
And they all go marching down
to the ground, to get out of the rain.
Boom, Boom, Boom,
Boom, Boom, Boom, Boom.

The ants go marching 5 by 5, hur-rah, hurrah.
The ants go marching 5 by 5, hur-rah, hurrah.
The ants go marching 5 by 5, the lit-tle one stopped to *(choose one)*:
    look at a hive; go for a drive.
And they all go marching down
to the ground, to get out of the rain.
Boom, Boom, Boom,
Boom, Boom, Boom, Boom.

The ants go marching 6 by 6, hur-rah, hurrah.
The ants go marching 6 by 6, hur-rah, hurrah.
The ants go marching 6 by 6, the lit-tle one stopped to *(choose one)*:
    build with bricks; pick up sticks.
And they all go marching down
to the ground, to get out of the rain.
Boom, Boom, Boom,
Boom, Boom, Boom, Boom.

The ants go marching 7 by 7, hurrah, hurrah.
The ants go marching 7 by 7, hurrah, hurrah.

The ants go marching 7 by 7 the little one stopped to *(choose one)*:

pray to heaven; count to eleven.

And they all go marching down
to the ground, to get out of the rain.
Boom, Boom, Boom,
Boom, Boom, Boom, Boom.

The ants go marching 8 by 8, hurrah, hurrah.
The ants go marching 8 by 8, hurrah, hurrah.
The ants go marching 8 by 8, the little one stopped to *(choose one)*:

shut the gate; fill his plate.

And they all go marching down
to the ground, to get out of the rain.
Boom, Boom, Boom,
Boom, Boom, Boom, Boom.

The ants go marching 9 by 9, hurrah, hurrah.

The ants go marching 9 by 9, hurrah, hurrah.
The ants go marching 9 by 9, the little one stopped to *(choose one)*:

draw a line; make a sign.

And they all go marching down
to the ground, to get out of the rain.
Boom, Boom, Boom,
Boom, Boom, Boom, Boom.

The ants go marching 10 by 10, hurrah, hurrah.

The ants go marching 10 by 10, hurrah, hurrah.
The ants go marching 10 by 10, the little one stopped to *(choose one)*:

say "The End!"; sing it again.

And they all go marching down
to the ground, to get out of the rain.
Boom, Boom, Boom,
Boom, Boom, Boom, Boom.

Activities

1. Finish the drawing. After the children have enjoyed singing the song, give each child a copy of the worksheet on page 33 and a crayon, pencil or marker. Show them how to write each number by starting at the star and following the pattern. Some numbers four, five and nine are written in two steps. Emphasize to the children that they should lift their pencil off the page and restart at the second star to finish writing the rest of the number.

2. Enjoy some nonfiction books together about ants. How many body parts does an ant have? How many legs do ants have? What different jobs do ants do? Where do ants live?

3. For a snack, make "ants on a log." Using a plastic knife, help children spread peanut butter on a stalk of celery. (Check for peanut allergies first.) Then let them count how many ants (raisins) they put on their log.

4. Make ants using cotton swabs. Show children how to dip their swab in black or brown paint. Encourage them to make three dots close together on their paper because ants have three body parts. When the paint is dry, children can draw six legs on each ant.

5. Make an ant using three raisins and some toothpicks. Put all three raisins on one toothpick. Then stick shorter toothpicks into the raisins for the ant's legs. Grapes or prunes may also be used to make a larger ant. Small styrofoam balls may be substituted for food items if desired.

6. Display two-part ant poster during this event (included on pp. 34–35). They may also be handed out to children for them to color.

The Ants Go Marching

Name _____

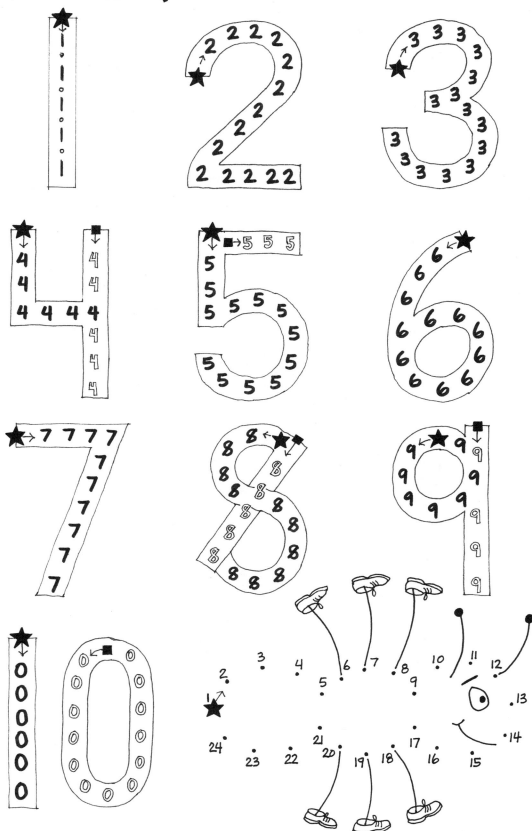

From *Top Dot Tales*. Copyright © 2001 by Valerie Marsh (Alleyside Press)

The Ants Go Marching

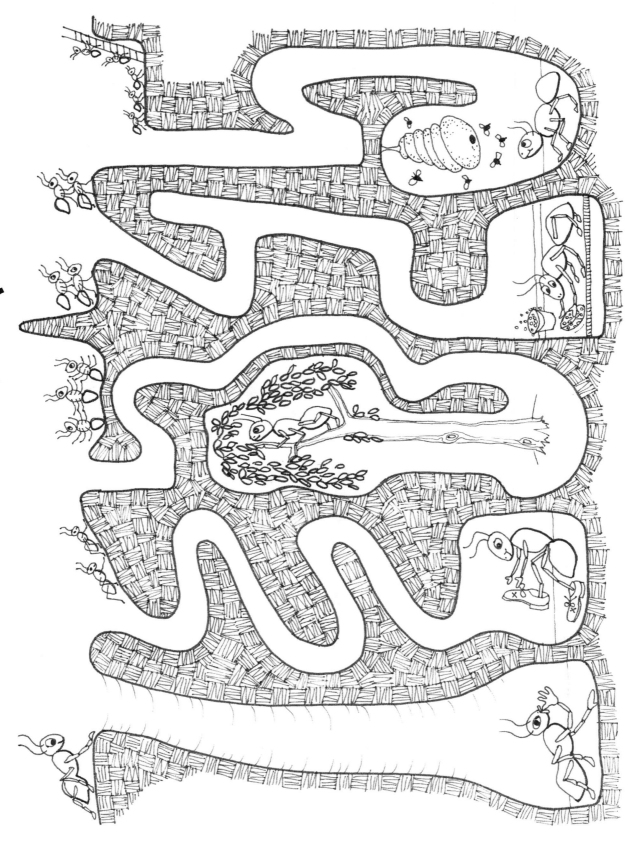

    From *Top Dot Tales*. Copyright © 2001 by Valerie Marsh (Alleyside Press)

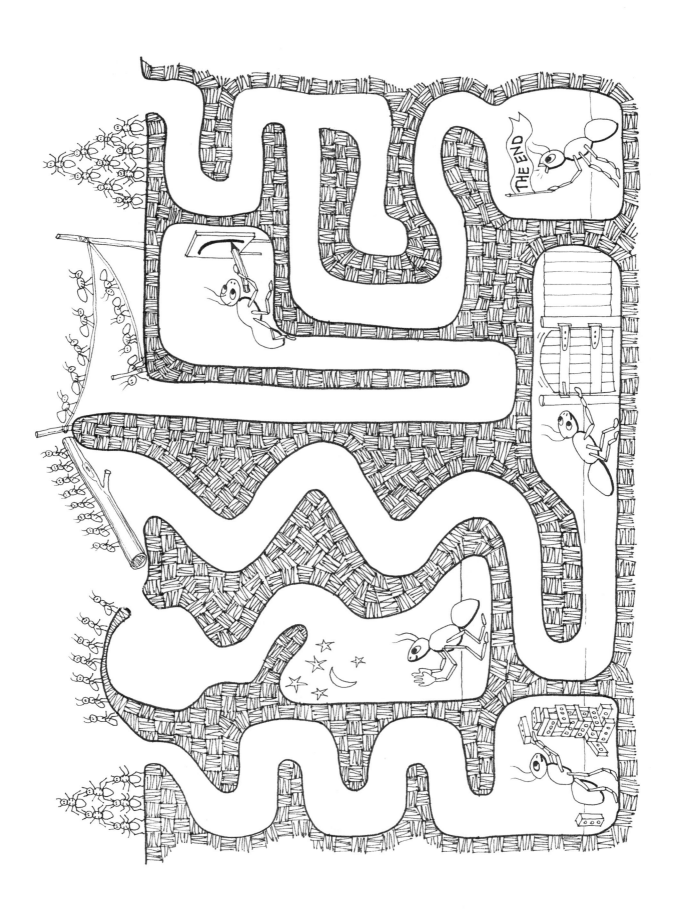

From *Top Dot Tales*. Copyright © 2001 by Valerie Marsh (Alleyside Press)

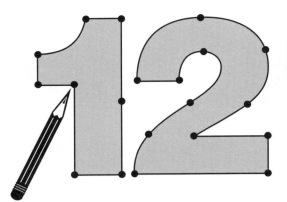

Down by the Bay

Down by the bay,
Where the watermelons grow.
Back to my home, I dare not go.
For if I do, my mother will say,
"Did you ever see a snail
wiggling it's tail?"
Down by the bay.

Down by the bay,
Where the watermelons grow.
Back to my home, I dare not go.
For if I do, my mother will say,
"Did you ever see a dog
kissing a frog?"
Down by the bay.

Down by the bay,
Where the watermelons grow.
Back to my home, I dare not go.

For if I do, my mother will say,
"Did you ever see a mouse
sitting on a house?"
Down by the bay.

Down by the bay,
Where the watermelons grow.
Back to my home, I dare not go.
For if I do, my mother will say,
"Did you ever see a snake,
eating a cake?"
Down by the bay.

Down by the bay,
Where the watermelons grow.
Back to my home, I dare not go.
For if I do, my mother will say,
"Did you ever have a time
when you couldn't make a rhyme?"
Down by the bay.

Activities

1. Sing the song. After singing the song, encourage children to trace the dotted lines and then color the pictures if they wish.

2. Discuss the rhyming words. Help the children think of other words to rhyme with the words in the song. "Snail," "tail," "pail," "mail." "Dog," "frog," "log," "hog," "jog." "Mouse," "house," "louse." "Snake," "cake," "rake," "bake," "wake." Let them pick one other word that rhymes with each set and color it in the correct box.

3. Make up your own verses. Children can think up other pairs of rhyming words to sing in this song. Some children might need a hint or two. For example, what could a bear do? Could he sit in a ......? (chair) Where could a car drive? Could it drive to a ......? (star)

4. Draw your own. Using simple outlines from "how-to-cartoon" books, or clip art programs, help children choose or draw two pictures that rhyme. They could then draw or copy the pictures and color in dots around the outline of the pictures. Finally, they could add numbers or letters to go with their dots.

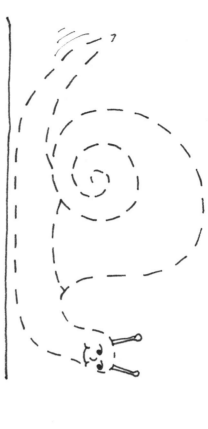

Name _____

From *Top Dot Tales*. Copyright © 2001 by Valerie Marsh (Alleyside Press)

13 The Farmer in the Dell

Sing this song several times before doing the drawing activity that goes with it. Explain that "takes" means "chooses," and a "dell" is a valley.

The farmer in the dell,
The farmer in the dell,
Hi ho, away we go,
The farmer in the dell.

The farmer takes a wife,
The farmer takes a wife,
Hi ho, away we go,
The farmer takes a wife.

The wife takes a child,
The wife takes a child,
Hi ho, away we go,
The wife takes a child.

The child takes a dog,
The child takes a dog,
Hi ho, away we go,
The child takes a dog.

The dog takes a cat,
The dog takes a cat,
Hi ho, away we go,
The dog takes a cat.

The cat takes a rat,
The cat takes a rat,
Hi ho, away we go,
The cat takes a rat.

The rat takes the cheese,
The rat takes the cheese,
Hi ho, away we go,
The rat takes the cheese.

The cheese stands alone,
The cheese stands alone,
Hi ho, away we go,
The cheese stands alone.

Activities

1. Sing the song with the children holding hands to form a circle.

2. Connect the dots on the picture. Point out that the pictures themselves form a circle. Encourage the children to complete the drawing by connecting the dots for each figure.

3. Change the song. Have fun with a rhyming words variation, such as:
   The frog hops on a log…; The bear sits in a chair…; The boy plays with a toy.
   Encourage the children to think up other rhyming word pairs to sing.

4. Make puppets. Enlarge the figures in the drawing and then photocopy one figure for each child. Let the children color and cut out the figures and glue them on heavy paper. Tape a popsicle stick or straw to the back of the puppet. Or children may tape their puppets on their shirts and act the song out. They may also use their puppets for other plays or activities.

Name _____

The Farmer in the Dell

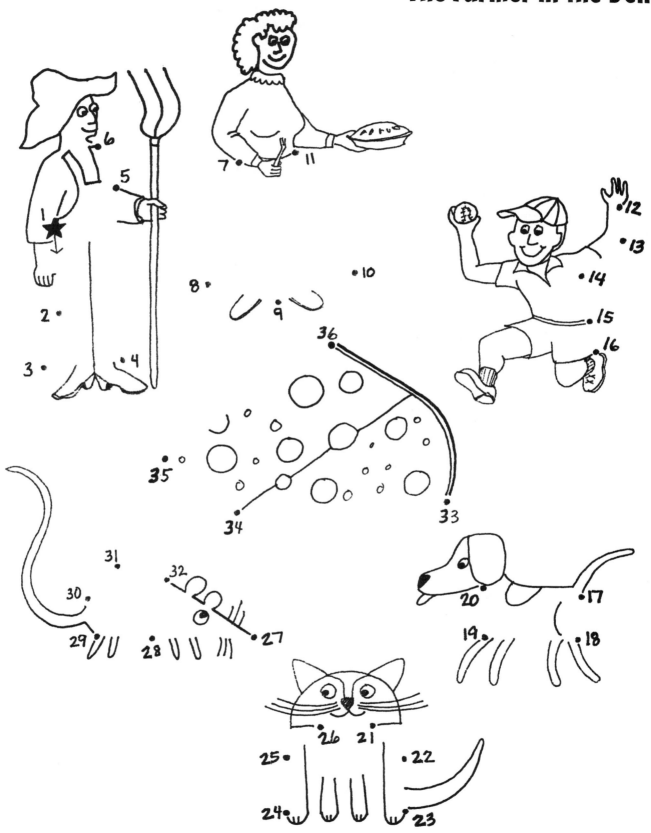

From *Top Dot Tales*. Copyright © 2001 by Valerie Marsh (Alleyside Press)

Fuzzy Wuzzy

Recite the poem several times with the children before they start drawing.

Fuzzy Wuzzy was a bear.
(Draw the bear's head. Start at the star. Draw from A to M.)

Fuzzy Wuzzy had no hair.
(Draw the bear's body. Start at the circle. Draw from 1–15.)

Fuzzy Wuzzy wasn't fuzzy, Was he?

Let's draw the bear's ears. What shapes do you see on the bear's ears? Yes, the ears have triangles and circles on them, don't they? Do you notice that they make a pattern? Trace over the pattern with your crayon. Let's say the pattern together: triangle, circle, triangle, circle, triangle.... Notice that there is a pattern on the bear's legs and arms. This pattern has three shapes, doesn't it? Let's say this pattern together—square, circle, triangle, square, circle, and triangle. Trace over it with your crayon.

Activities

1. Color patterns. After discussing the patterns again with the children, encourage them to color the pattern. For the bear's ears, have children use two differently colored crayons or markers. Then show them how to color the circle one color and the triangle the other color. They should follow the pattern and use alternate colors. For the bear's legs and arms, three colors are needed.

2. Count teddy bears. Give each child a handful of teddy bear cookies. Let everyone count their cookies. Make a game of eating the cookies. "One teddy bear went into a dark cave. (Children pop one cookie into their mouth. *Check for food allergies first!*) Now how many teddy bears are left?" Eat cookies in groups of ones and twos, counting the remaining bears each time.

3. Read teddy bear books. Ask each child to name a favorite book. Make a bar graph, allowing each child to color a specific box. Then count and compare the number of votes each book received.

4. Enjoy a teddy bear puppet. If a teddy bear puppet is not available, it is easy to make one. Cut a slit in the back of a old teddy bear. Then carefully remove enough stuffing so that your hand can fit inside the bear and your fingers can fit inside the bear's arms. Let your new teddy bear puppet lead the children in saying "Fuzzy Wuzzy" again faster and faster and faster.

5. Challenge activity: Help Fuzzy Wuzzy reach the honey on the other side of the maze! (See worksheet on page 42.)

Fuzzy Wuzzy

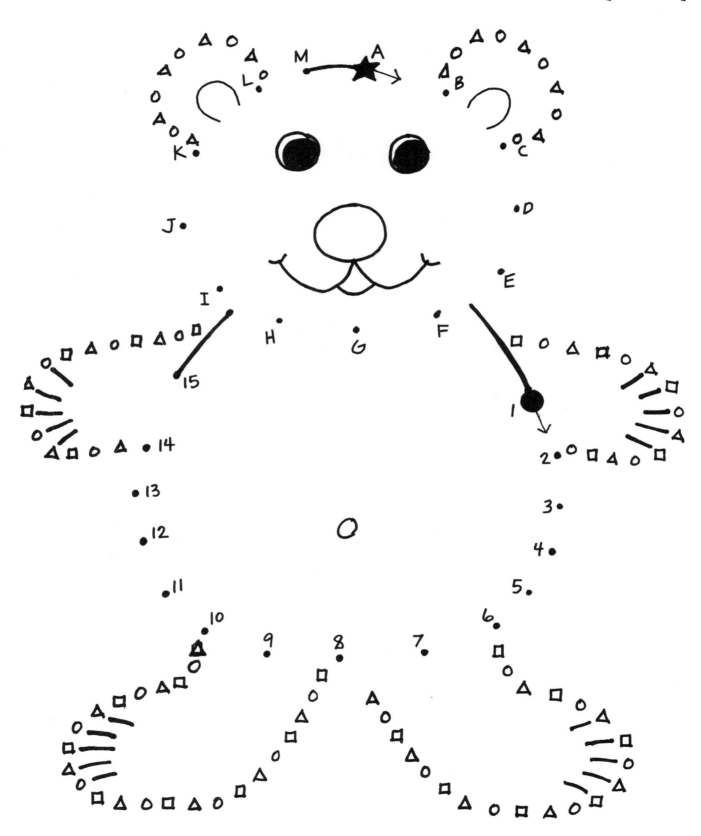

From *Top Dot Tales*. Copyright © 2001 by Valerie Marsh (Alleyside Press)

Bear Maze

Name _____

 From *Top Dot Tales.* Copyright © 2001 by Valerie Marsh (Alleyside Press)

Coyote and the Marshmallows

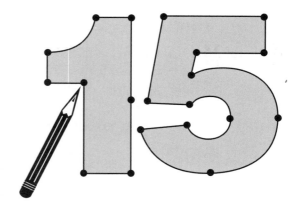

Have you ever had a campfire and roasted hot dogs or marshmallows? It's fun, isn't it? This is a story about a campfire.

One summer evening, six rabbit friends decided to have a campfire. They loved to sit around the fire in a big circle. *(Look at the ring of small circles inside the ring of big Xs. With your crayon, connect the small circles to make one larger circle.)*

Their favorite food to roast was a giant head of lettuce. Do you think that you would like to eat roasted lettuce? No, neither would I, but the rabbits loved roasted lettuce!

When the six rabbits roasted lettuce heads, Coyote never bothered them. He did not like lettuce. But if the six friends roasted another food, they kept their ears pricked up, and listened for Coyote's soft, sneaky footsteps. What other kinds of foods do you think that the rabbits roasted on their campfire? *(Accept all answers.)*

One of their favorite foods to roast was marshmallows. Unfortunately for the six rabbit friends, marshmallows were also Coyote's favorite food. He could smell those marshmallows roasting from miles away, and he would come running! Sometimes the rabbits thought that Coyote could even hear them getting out their roasting sticks—he was that quick. *(Draw the rabbits' roasting sticks by tracing the dashed line from big X to the small X.)*

The six rabbits knew that if they were roasting marshmallows, Coyote was probably hiding behind some nearby bushes, just waiting for those marshmallows to get nice and toasty.

Then Coyote would sneak out from behind the bushes, howling and barking at the top of his lungs. He would race around and grab all the marshmallows off the rabbits' roasting sticks, stuffing all of the marshmallows into his mouth.

The six rabbit friends got awfully mad at Coyote for stealing their marshmallows, so they decided to play a trick on Coyote. One night, they built an extra big campfire. Each rabbit put a nice, big marshmallow at the end of his or her stick.

Then the six rabbits started to roast their marshmallows. They pretended not to notice Coyote hiding behind the bushes. At the very moment when the marshmallows were done and Coyote jumped from behind the bushes, the rabbits pulled their trick. All the rabbits lifted their sticks as high in the air as their little rabbit paws could reach. Then they flipped their sticks as hard as they could. What do you think happened to the marshmallows? That's right, all of the marshmallows flew off the end of their sticks and flew right up into the sky.

You know how sticky marshmallows are, don't you? These marshmallows were so very sticky that they stuck all over the night sky. *(Look at the three dots in-between each roasting stick. Connect the three dots to make a triangle.)*

You know, those marshmallows are still there today. They are the small, white twinkles in the night sky. Do you know what we call them? Yes, we call them stars. Now take a look at your drawing. Did you draw a star?

Activities

1. For visual effect, show the listeners a roasting stick and then put a marshmallow on it at the appropriate point in the story.

2. Eat some marshmallows. (Always check for food allergies.) At the end of the story, give each listener a marshmallow to eat. Before handing out the marshmallows, let the children help you count out how many marshmallows you will need. How many are left in the bag? Is there enough for everyone to have a second marshmallow?

3. Learn more about stars. Show that children several nonfiction books about stars. Ask the children if they think that stars are really made of marshmallows. Discuss astronomers and their jobs.

4. Make stars. Give each child a previously cut out star. (Use a die cut machine if available.) Let each child decorate his or her star using markers, glitter, sequins or hole punches.

5. Challenge activity: Help coyote get through the maze to the rabbit and marshmallows (see worksheet on page 46).

Name _____

Coyote and the Marshmallows

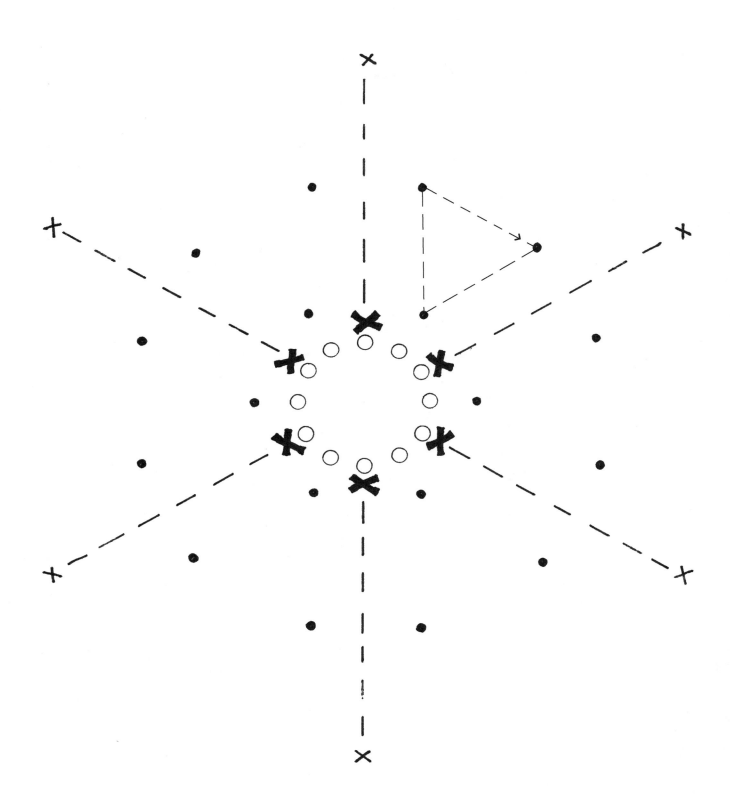

From *Top Dot Tales*. Copyright © 2001 by Valerie Marsh (Alleyside Press)

Coyote Maze

 From *Top Dot Tales*. Copyright © 2001 by Valerie Marsh (Alleyside Press)

Frog's Trick

Once there was a lion who expected all of the other animals to bring him breakfast each morning. But when Frog's turn came, she woke up late and did not have time to get any food for Lion.

Lion roared, "Frog, where is my breakfast?"

Frog said, "Well, I don't have anything for you to eat this morning, Lion."

Lion roared, "Then I shall eat you, dear Frog."

Frog thought fast and answered, "Oh, don't eat me. It is not my fault that I don't have your breakfast. It was stolen as I was hopping over here with it."

Lion roared, "Who stole my breakfast? I will get him for this."

Frog answered, "Oh, come and see, Lion. I will show you who stole your breakfast. He had long hair, yellow eyes, and sharp teeth just like yours. He was by my pond." And Frog started hopping back to her pond.

When Lion and Frog arrived at his pond, Frog pretended to look all around. Then Frog said, "I don't see him anywhere. Maybe he is hiding."

Frog pointed to the bottom of the pond and said, "Look, there he is. He has eaten your breakfast and now he is hiding."

Lion walked over to the pond and looked in. He saw a big lion with shaggy hair, yellow eyes, and sharp teeth. He roared and jumped into the water to get him. *Splash!!*

As Frog hopped away, Lion realized that he had been tricked. "I was looking at my own reflection in the pond. There is no other lion," Lion said. "From now on, I am going to get my own breakfast."

Activities

1. Retell the story. Discuss how Frog tricked Lion. Discuss the meaning of reflection and let everyone look at their reflection in a hand mirror or classroom mirror.

2. Connect the dots, counting by fives. Then have children draw Lion's reflection in the pond.

3. Draw a reflection. Encourage the children to look at themselves in a mirror and draw a picture using their reflection. Show them Norman Rockwell's famous painting of himself looking in a mirror and painting. If the children would rather draw a reflection of something or someone else, let them try it.

4. Make reflection pictures with paint. Have children trace and cut a simple outline of a butterfly. Then let them dab on paint with a cotton swab on one side only. Children should then fold their butterfly in half and rub the sides together. This will transfer the paint to the other side. When they open up their butterflies, they have a reflection!

Frog's Trick

Name _____

 From *Top Dot Tales*. Copyright © 2001 by Valerie Marsh (Alleyside Press)

The Lion and the Mouse

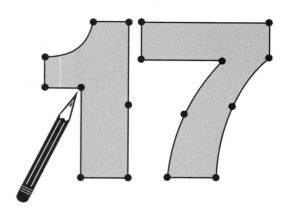

One day, a little mouse found a great big acorn. She said, "Wow! I am going to take this wonderful acorn home to eat." The little mouse picked it up in her tiny mouth and started carrying it home.

The nut was so very big that it stuck quite far out of her mouth, and she could not see exactly where she was going. And though the mouse tried to be very careful, she tripped over something and fell down. That something that she tripped over was not a rock or a tree root. No, it was the foot of a big lion who had been taking a nap.

The lion woke up and put his paw on the tail of the mouse. Then he roared, "How dare you wake me up?"

The mouse timidly replied, "I am so sorry that I woke you up. Please let me go. Here, you can have this big acorn that I was going to eat."

The lion roared, "I do not eat acorns. I eat fat, juicy field mice like you."

The mouse said, "Please, Mr. Lion, if you would be so kind as to let me go, I will repay your kindness someday."

The lion laughed again and roared, "I will let you go. But I will not need your help. Take your acorn and be off with you."

A few days later, the mouse heard the lion roaring but this time his roar sounded afraid. She followed the sound of the lion's roar and saw that the lion was trapped in a hunter's net.

The mouse said, "Oh, Mr. Lion, I can help you. Stand still and I will free you."

The lion roared, "You cannot free me. This net is so strong that not even I can break the ropes."

The mouse replied, "Remember that day that I tripped over your foot and woke you up? I said that someday I would help you. Be still and let me help you get free of this net."

The lion stood still and the mouse began to gnaw on the ropes. She chewed through just enough ropes to permit the lion to squeeze out through the hole. He was free. The lion said, "Thank you so much little mouse! Now I must be off before the hunters come back." He ran off into the high grasses, and never again ate mice.

Activities

1. Review the story. Discuss the trusting kindness of the mouse before the children connect the dots.

2. Connect the dots to make the hunter's net. First, start at the star and connect A to B to C, and so on through the alphabet. Then, starting at the circle, connect 1 to 2 to 3, and so on through to 10.

3. Make puppets. Children can color and cut out the lion and mouse. (You may wish to enlarge them first.) Then they can glue them onto a straw or popsicle stick. Use a piece of a fruit bag as a net and put on a play.

4. Learn more about lions and mice. Borrow some nonfiction books from the library and find out where lions and mice live and what they eat.

5. Make a food puppet lion. Cut an apple crosswise in half and put it on a plate. Use squirt cheese for the mane. Using a dab of cheese, stick raisins or olives on for eyes. Use toothpicks for whiskers.

The Lion and the Mouse

Name _____

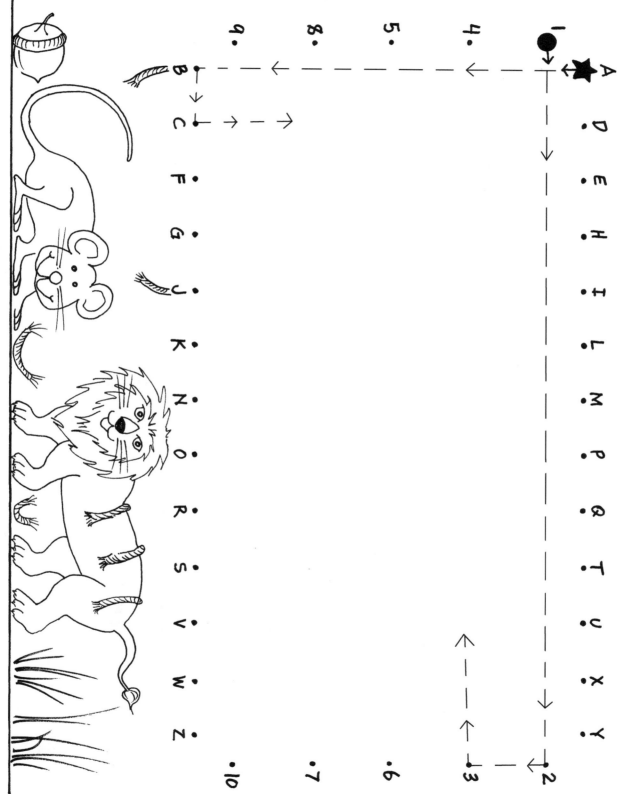

WOOD DALE DISTRICT LIBRARY
WOOD DALE ILLINOIS

Three Silly Wishes

Far ago a farmer took a walk in the forest. It was a fine day. As he walked, he enjoyed watching the golden leaves float down from their branches. Each tree along the path was prettier than the last, and so he walked from tree to tree. He did not pay any attention to which paths he turned on and before he knew it, he had walked much farther than he had planned. He realized he was lost. But just then, he heard a small voice.

"Help me, help me! Over here, I'm over here, I'm stuck," said a tiny voice.

The farmer looked all around him to find out where the tiny voice was coming from. Then he noticed a large tree limb that had fallen across the path.

The voice said, "Oh, please, this limb is so heavy. Lift it off of me. Quickly!"

Using all of his strength, the farmer was able to lift the limb just enough so that whoever was calling could crawl out. Who do you think was under the limb?

It was a little elf! She dusted herself off and said, "Oh, thank you so much. I really do appreciate it. Is there anything I can do to help you since you helped me?"

The farmer said, "I wish you could help me. I have lost my way. I wish you could tell me the way home."

"That I can," said the elf. "That I can."

"How can you? You don't even know where I live," asked the farmer.

The elf said, "Perhaps you noticed that I am an elf. We elves know these things. I will show you your path home and I will also give you three wishes."

The farmer said, "Three wishes, what do you mean, three wishes?"

The elf answered, "Just exactly that. You may have three wishes. Whatever you wish for will be granted immediately. So be very, very careful what you wish for. And thank you again for lifting the tree limb off me. Now here is your path home, and remember, be careful what you wish for." The elf pointed to a path and then turned and vanished into the woods.

The farmer started off on the path that the elf told him to travel. As he walked along, he thought of all the things that he might want to wish for.

He finally arrived home, and when his wife saw him coming up the walk, she stepped out of the door and said, "What happened? You look so excited."

The farmer answered, "Oh, you will never believe this, but I just met an elf and she granted me three wishes."

His wife answered, "An elf granted you three wishes? You are right, I do not believe you."

The farmer answered, "Well, she did. Did you fix supper? I just realized how hungry I am. I walked a long way in the woods."

The wife answered, "No, I did not make any supper. The day was too nice to be inside cooking. I have been outside, enjoying this weather."

The farmer answered, "Oh, I am so hungry. I wish that we could eat supper right now!"

Do you know what happened next? Yes, immediately a huge table appeared right before their very eyes, right in their front yard. And the table was filled with all sorts of good things to eat!

The wife said, "Oh, my! You wished for dinner and now there it is. You really did have three wishes. But, you were so stupid. You just wasted a wish on one dinner when you could have wished that everyone in the world could eat dinner tonight! Or at least a bigger house! That was really a dumb wish!"

"I am so sorry. I just didn't think. I will be more careful with my next two wishes. Here, let's eat," said the farmer and he reached for a big round sausage.

But his wife yelled, "How can you eat at a time like this? You just wasted a wish and now you are going to forget all about it and eat that sausage like nothing happened? You should let me make the wish next time. I would never wish for anything as silly as dinner!"

The farmer felt himself getting angry as he replied, "I said I was sorry. Now please, just sit down and eat. This sausage is delicious. Would you like to try some?"

"No, I do not want any sausage! I want that wish back! How can you eat sausage at a time like this?" yelled the wife.

By now the farmer was so angry that he shouted, "I wish that this sausage would stick to your nose! Forever!"

Do you know what happened next? Yes, that fat sausage stuck to the wife's nose. What do you think she did next? Yes, she tried to pull it off of her nose. Could she pull the sausage off her nose? No, it was stuck fast.

Her husband started laughing! She looked so funny with a great big sausage hanging from her nose. But then he realized that it was really not very funny at all and he said, "Oh, no! I am really sorry about your nose. And I just wasted another wish, didn't I? Here, let me help you get that sausage off your nose." He pulled and pulled on that sausage as hard as he could. Do you think that he could get the sausage off? No, he could not pull it off either.

Then he said, "There is only one way to get the sausage off of your nose. I will have to use my last wish and wish it off."

His wife yelled, "Hurry up and do it! I do not want to have this sausage stuck on my nose one minute longer."

What do you think happened next? Yes, he used up his last wish and said, "I wish that sausage to be gone from your nose, now."

The sausage disappeared from her nose and so did the all of their wishes! After they thought about it for a minute, they both realized how silly their wishes had been. They laughed about their lost wishes, mostly to keep themselves from crying. And then they sat down and ate the nice, big dinner.

Activities

1. Connect the dots. Have children connect the dots 1–13 for the elf, then color in the rest of the picture.

2. Discuss the story. Can you name all three wishes? Why was the wife so angry?

3. Enjoy other versions. Find versions of this story. Compare and contrast several versions.

4. Find number three. Many fairy tales have the number three in them. Name some with the children. (*The Three Pigs, The Three Bears, The Three Billy Goats, The Magic Fish*)

5. If you could have three wishes, what would you wish for?

Name _____

From *Top Dot Tales*. Copyright © 2001 by Valerie Marsh (Alleyside Press)

Five Little Monkeys and Mr. Alligator

Five little monkeys swinging in a tree,
Teasing Mr. Alligator, "You can't catch me! You can't catch me!"
Along came Mr. Alligator and...
SNAP!!!(Clap hands together loudly.)

Four little monkeys swinging in a tree,
Teasing Mr. Alligator, "You can't catch me! You can't catch me!"
Along came Mr. Alligator and...
SNAP!!! (Clap hands together loudly.)

Three little monkeys swinging in a tree,
Teasing Mr. Alligator, "You can't catch me! You can't catch me!"
Along came Mr. Alligator and...
SNAP!!! (Clap hands together loudly.)

Two little monkeys swinging in a tree,
Teasing Mr. Alligator, "You can't catch me! You can't catch me!"
Along came Mr. Alligator and...
SNAP!!! (Clap hands together loudly.)

One little monkey swinging in a tree,
Teasing Mr. Alligator, "You can't catch me! You can't catch me!"
Along came Mr. Alligator and...
SNAP!!! (Clap hands together loudly.)

No little monkeys swinging in a tree,
Teasing Mr. Alligator, "You can't catch me! You can't catch me!"
Along came Mr. Alligator and...
BURP!! BURP!! BURP!! BURP!! BURP!!

Then there were.....
Five little monkeys swinging in a tree,
Teasing Mr. Alligator, "You can't catch me! You can't catch me."
Along came Mr. Alligator and
SNAP!!! (Clap hands together loudly.)

Activities

1. Finish the drawing. After everyone has enjoyed this poem, encourage the children to connect the dots on the alligator. Have the children identify and trace the numbers on the monkeys. Ask the children to draw teeth in the alligator's mouth.

2. Learn sign language. Using the illustrations below, show the children how to make the signs for "monkey," "tree," "alligator," "can't," "catch," and "me." Then recite the poem again adding in the signs for these words.

3. Learn more about alligators. Share some nonfiction books with the children.

4. Make an alligator snack. Help children spread peanut butter on a piece of celery and then stick small triangular shaped chips into the peanut butter. (Always check for food allergies.) This represents the alligator's back. Put a dab of peanut butter at both ends of the celery stick and then place pretzel sticks in the peanut butter for the legs. Use raisins for eyes.

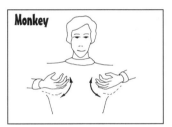

Monkey

Claw shape both hands, then scratch sides of chest twice.

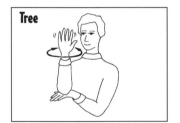

Tree

Place back of LH under R elbow. Rapidly twist and shake RH "5" shape.

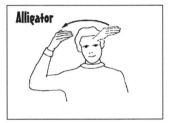

Alligator

"5"-shape hands together, with fingers pointing out. Open hands widely like an alligator mouth.

Can't

"1"-shape hands, palms down. Strike tip of LH index with tip of RH index, passing down.

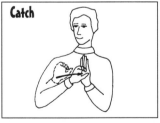

Catch

LH open, palm facing right. Hit LH palm with index and thumb of RH "C"-shape.

Me

Touch chest with index finger.

Five Little Monkeys and Mr. Alligator

Name _____

From *Top Dot Tales*. Copyright © 2001 by Valerie Marsh (Alleyside Press)

Rabbit and Snake

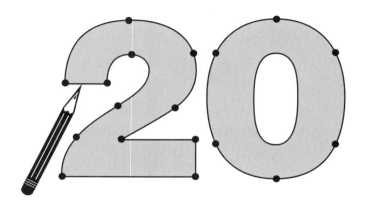

One day Snake was tired of slithering around in the hot sun. He decided to take a break in the shade of a pile of rocks. He had just settled down for a cool snooze in the shade when a big rock tumbled off the pile of rocks. The rock clattered down the pile and rolled right on Snake's back. Snake wiggled and squirmed, but he could not get out from under the heavy rock.

Just then, Rabbit hopped by. Snake yelled, "Hey there, Rabbit, old buddy, old pal, old friend of mine! How are you doing today?"

Rabbit replied, "I am doing just great. But you, Snake, on the other hand, don't look so good. That rock looks mighty heavy. How'd it end up on your back?"

Snake said, "Oh, this little old rock. Why, I put it there myself. It helps me relax after a long, hard day."

Rabbit said, "A long hard day, right. All you do is chase me around, trying to eat me. Looks like as long as that rock is on your back, I won't have to be running from you."

Snake said, "Well, Rabbit, you always have been pretty smart, and I see that you figured out that this rock is just a bit heavy on my back. Perhaps you could kindly take it off of me."

Rabbit said, "Oh, no, Snake. I am smarter than that. If I removed the rock from your back, you would be chasing me down for your lunch again."

Snake said, "Oh, I promise I will never chase you again, really. And I will never try to eat you either. Please just get this rock off of me. Please."

Rabbit said, "Snake, you are always going to be a snake. That means that you will always be chasing me for lunch. That's your job. And me, I am always going to be a rabbit. That means I am always going to be running away from you. That's my job. But as long as that heavy rock is holding you down, you get a break from chasing and I get a break from running. What a deal for both of us!"

And Rabbit hopped off, leaving Snake with the rock on his back.

Activities

1. Count by fives. After sharing this story with the children, practice counting by fives. A fun way to do this is to have everyone hold their hands up in the air. Then count each hand by fives to discover how many fingers there are all together. Writing the numbers on a marker board as you count by fives is a great way for children to learn number recognition. Showing the number flashcard is also a great way to visually reinforce counting by fives.

2. Discuss the story. Why did Snake say that the rock wasn't really heavy? Why did Rabbit refuse to help the snake? When Rabbit said that Snake got a break from chasing him, was it really a good deal for Snake?

3. Connect the dots. When the children have picked up the pattern of counting by fives, have them draw their snake. They may wish to color a pattern or design on their snake. Children can then trace the rock and rabbit.

4. Make more snakes. Create snakes using play dough or modeling clay. Encourage them to put a small ball of clay on the table. Then show the children how to use the palm of their hand to roll the clay on the table into a snake. Children may also roll a ball of clay between the palms of their hands to make a snake.

5. Make a rattlesnake. Give each child a long business envelope and encourage them to draw a snake on it. Then give them a handful of popcorn seeds, paper clips, beans, or small candies to put in their envelope. After they seal the envelope, they are ready to rattle their snake!

Name _____

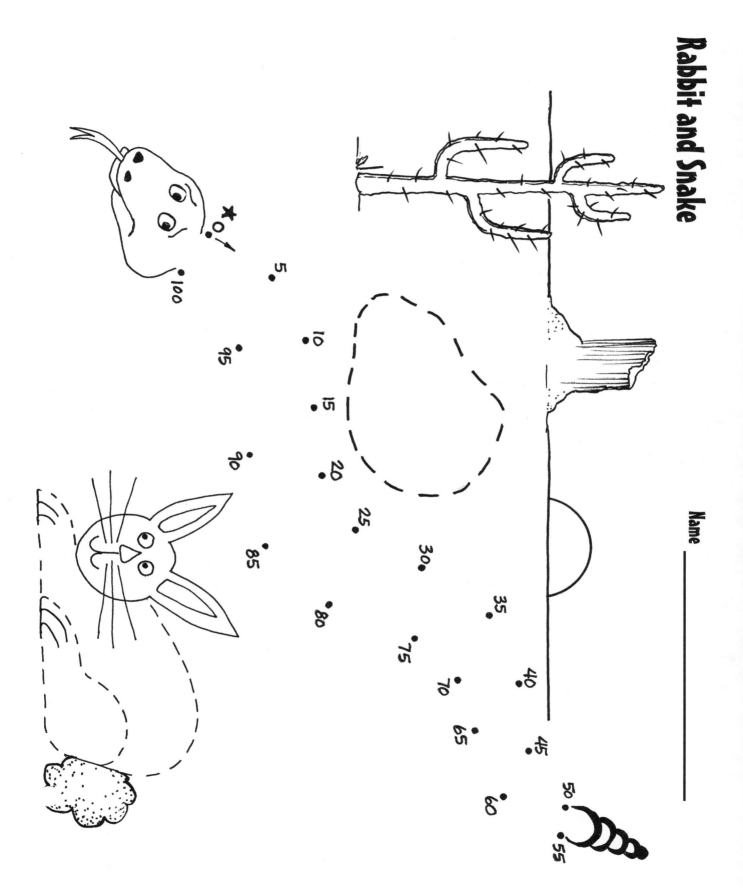

From *Top Dot Tales*. Copyright © 2001 by Valerie Marsh (Alleyside Press)

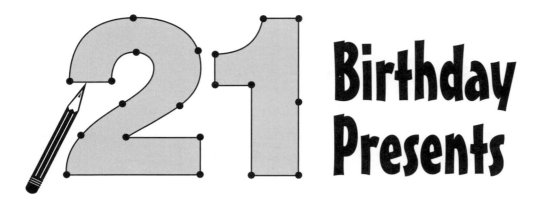

Birthday Presents

Matt wanted to get a present for his Grandmother's birthday. She was special to him, and her birthday was on a special day. Her birthday was on the first day of spring! Do you know what day the first day of spring is on? It is on March 21.

Matt said to himself, "What can I give her? I do not have any money to buy her a present, but I do want to give her a really neat gift. I think I will just walk over to her house and ask her what she wants."

Matt started walking on the path that led through the fields to her house. *(Start at the star and trace Matt's path with your finger or crayon.)*

Along the way, he noticed that there were lots of beautiful spring flowers that were just blooming. He had walked on this path many times before, but he had never noticed so many flowers. *(Why do you think there are lots of flowers now? Yes, because it is spring.)*

Matt leaned over to smell the flowers and said to himself, "Look at these beautiful wildflowers. I bet Grandma would really like some." So Matt picked some of the flowers as he walked along. *(Trace the large, dashed flower in the center.)*

When he got to Grandma's house, she said, "Oh, Matt, are these for my birthday?! What a wonderful gift! Look at all the different colors of flowers! I love all their different smells! Did you come over here just to bring these to me?"

Matt said, "No, I mean yes. Well, actually, I walked over here because I wanted to ask you what you wanted for your birthday."

Grandma said quickly, "These flowers are just what I want for my birthday. In fact, I really needed some flowers just now."

Matt asked, "What do you mean, Grandma?"

Grandma replied, "Instead of telling you what I need these flowers for, I think that I will just surprise you instead. Let's go back to your house now. I think your mother is expecting us."

Matt and Grandma started off to his house. Only this time, they did not walk on the path through the woods, they decided to take the long way around. *(Starting at the circle, connect the dots 1–10.)* When they got to Matt's house, Grandma said, "Matt, show your mom the beautiful flowers you picked for me for my birthday."

Matt said, "Grandma, I didn't bring them. I thought you did."

Grandma said, "No, Matt, I thought you did. Well, would you please just run back and get them?"

Matt ran as fast as he could down the other path. *(Start at the triangle and trace Matt's path with your finger or crayon.)* When he got to Grandma's house, he picked up the flowers and decided to take the shortcut back home. *(Start at the square and connect the dots 11–20.)*

"Here are your flowers, Grandma," said Matt.

Grandma took the flowers and said, "Matt, your mother made me a birthday cake. Do you like it?" *(Trace over the dashed lines at the top, bottom and sides of the cake. Did you know that you were drawing a cake?)*

Matt said, "Your cake is nice, but it is rather plain. It needs some decorations on it."

Grandma said, "I know. That is why I needed the flowers. Watch this." Grandma placed the flowers on the sides of the cake and all around the edge of the cake. "Now my cake looks great! It is a Happy Birthday, Happy Spring Cake!" *(Trace the remaining dashed flowers on cake.)*

The flowers did make the cake look so pretty that Matt had to agree. He said, "Happy Birthday, Grandma! Happy Spring, everyone!"

Activities

1. Finish the cake. Children may wish to color the cake and draw flowers around the bottom of the cake. Add candles to the cake. Children can draw candles on their cake and color it if they wish.

2. Discuss birthdays. Ask the children to tell the date of their birthday, to describe their favorite birthday memory, and to tell how they like to celebrate their birthday.

3. Make a birthday card. Choose someone in the class, school, or community who is celebrating their birthday soon. Make a card that everyone can sign or let individuals make cards.

4. Serve a flower-decorated cake or cupcakes.

Birthday Presents

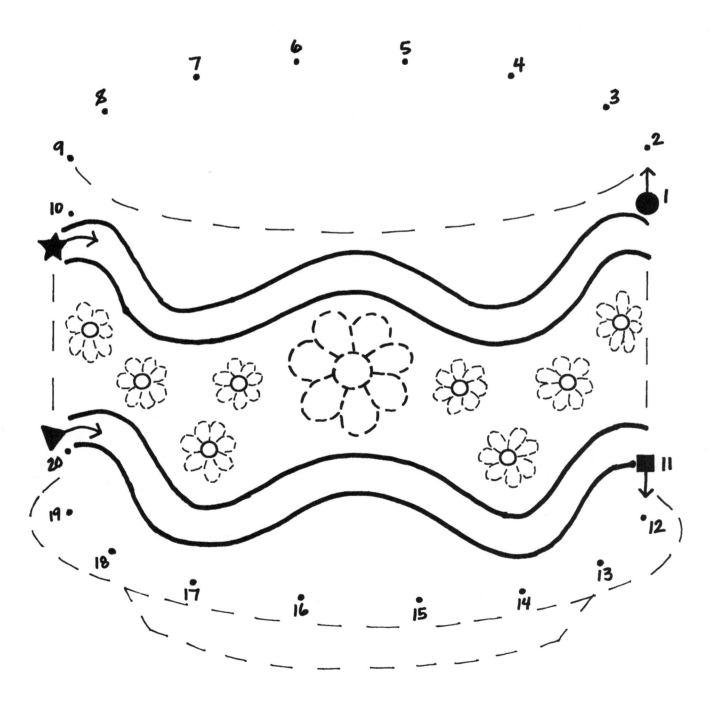

From *Top Dot Tales*. Copyright © 2001 by Valerie Marsh (Alleyside Press)

Valentine Wishes

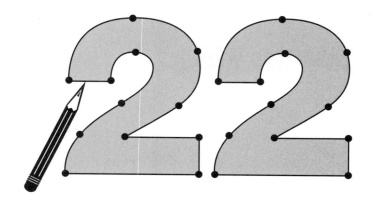

Sing slowly to the tune of "I'm A Little Teapot." Have children point to the letters as they sing them.

V - A - L - E - N - T - I - N - E
Here is my heart.
I give to you.
When you turn me over, then I shout,
I love you with all my heart.

Song Variation:

Clap instead of singing the letters. For the second verse, begin by clapping instead of singing the letter V. On the third verse, clap to represent the letter V and the letter A. One the fourth verse, clap for the letters V, A, and L. Continue until all the letters are clapped in the rhythm of the song, instead of being sung.

Activities

1. Draw the heart. Have the children first trace the numbers 1–100 and then use a marker to draw the heart. This more difficult task is made easier by the fact that the drawing is obvious.

2. Make more hearts. After the children have traced the hearts, let them cut them out and use them for a pattern to draw more hearts. Provide heart patterns of different sizes for children to trace. Children can make a collage with their heart tracings.

3. Paint hearts. Put cut-out hearts into an oatmeal box or plastic margarine tub. Place marbles in a tray filled with a small amount of red, pink, or white paint. Then spoon the paint-covered marbles into the container and put the lid on. Children can shake the container to "paint" their hearts. Rolling the paint-covered marbles over hearts placed in a box lid also works well and is not quite as noisy!

4. Make colored glue hearts. Cut a heart frame from red, pink, or purple paper. Then glue it onto a white sheet of paper. Drizzle different colors of glue inside the heart. (Colored glue can be purchased or made by mixing food coloring into the glue.)

Valentine Wishes

Name _____

From *Top Dot Tales.* Copyright © 2001 by Valerie Marsh (Alleyside Press)

St. Patrick's Day

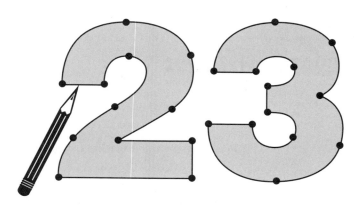

Have you ever heard the story that there is a pot of gold at the end of every rainbow? Well, Marie heard her Grandpa tell this story, and she decided that the next time she saw a rainbow she would go out and find the pot of gold.

Every time it rained, Marie looked up in the sky for a rainbow. Finally, one rainy day in the middle of March, she saw one. All the kids on her street saw it too. Marie said, "Come on, let's go find the end of the rainbow." *(Start at the star and draw from 1 to 10.)*

When they looked very closely at the rainbow, they decided that the end was probably in Renee's backyard. *(Draw from 10 to 50.)* The friends ran to Renee's house. But when the friends looked in her yard, the end of the rainbow wasn't there.

Maybe it was in Weston's backyard. The friends ran over to his yard and looked. Did the rainbow end there? *(Draw from 50 to 77.)* No, the end of the rainbow was not there.

The rainbow was starting to fade and the friends knew that they had to hurry. So, they ran to Celeste's house and looked in her backyard. *(Draw from 77 to 90.)* Do you think that they found the rainbow's end and the pot of gold there? No, they did not.

Finally the friends all walked back to Marie's house. *(Draw from 90–100.)* Marie said, "I am disappointed that we did not find the end of the rainbow and the pot of gold."

The sun was now shining brightly and the rainbow had disappeared. The friends all sat down in the grass to rest. Marie picked at the damp grass. Suddenly she said, "I did not find the pot of gold at the end of the rainbow but I did find something that will bring me good luck. Look at this!" (What did she find in the grass?)

Activities

1. Finish the picture. Let all the children have a chance to connect the dots and color the picture if they wish.

2. Count to one hundred. Using the numbers on the shamrock, count to one hundred together as a class. Extend this activity by using a Hundreds chart or by writing the numbers 1–100 on the board and helping the children follow along as you count. Point out the patterns.

3. Celebrate St. Patrick's Day. Learn more about rainbows, four-leaf clovers, and this holiday.

4. Discuss luck. Ask the children if they have any good luck beliefs of their own. Do they have a lucky number? Have they ever found a four-leaf clover?

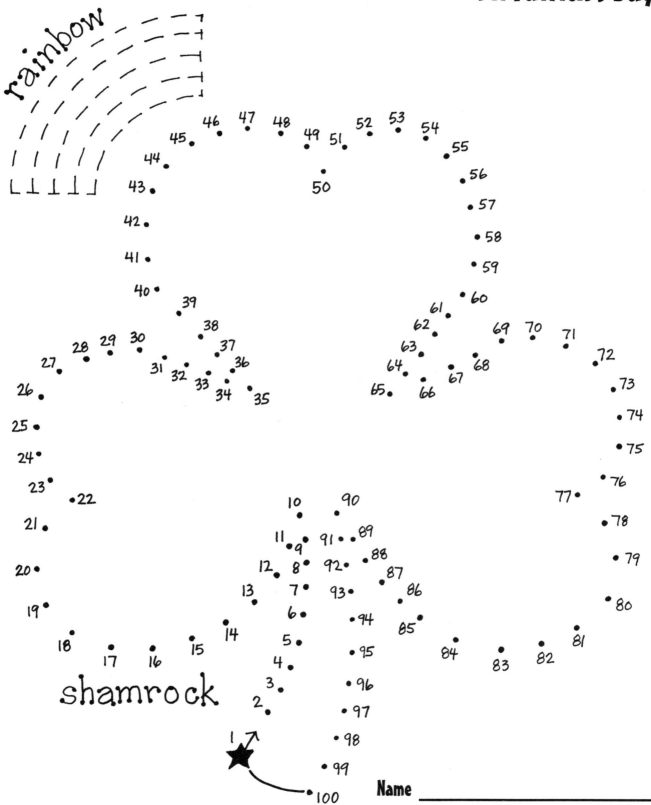

rainbow

shamrock

Name _____

From *Top Dot Tales*. Copyright © 2001 by Valerie Marsh (Alleyside Press)

Spring Rainbows

Long ago, there was a beautiful land called the Land of Many Flowers. Why do you think it was called this? Yes, because many beautiful flowers bloomed there.

One sunny day, hummingbirds were flitting from flower to flower.

One hummingbird said, "Winter is always so cold, and I do not like snow. I am glad to leave as soon as there is the tiniest hint of cold weather."

The flowers heard the birds and they asked each other, "Winter? We are tired of winter. Is winter coming around again? Already? We make the Earth such a beautiful place. But all too soon we are covered with a cold blanket of snow. We are no longer beautiful: in the cold, we become wilted and brown."

The Earth said, "The flowers are right. They are such an important part of our beautiful world. They make everything so beautiful in the spring and summer and even fall. Then when winter comes, they are covered up by snow. I need to do something about that. Let me think, hmmm… I know, I will make something beautiful from the flowers. It will be something everyone can see. I will put all the red flowers together in a long line, all the blue flowers together in a long line, and all the yellow flowers together in a long line. I will put these long lines of flowers next to each other, way up high in the sky where everyone can see them."

Today we can see these lines of color way up high in the sky. Do you know what the beautiful lines of flower colors together are called? Yes, they are called a "rainbow." Have you ever seen a rainbow?

When we look up in the sky and see a beautiful rainbow, we will remember that the colors of the rainbow are made up of all the pretty colors of spring and summer flowers.

Activities

1. Connect the dots. Let children connect the dots and then color the rainbow with markers or crayons.

2. Eat a rainbow. Choose foods that represent the colors of the rainbow. Children can eat strawberries or apple slices, blueberries, banana slices, both colors of grapes, and orange sections. Also try colored vegetables!

3. Make a rainbow. Set out scraps of colored paper and glue. Show children how to tear the paper into small pieces and glue on paper in the shape of a rainbow.

4. Enjoy some nonfiction books about weather and rainbows.

Name _____

Spring Rainbows

Earth Day

On April 22, we celebrate a special day. It is called "Earth Day." On this day, people take time to remember that the Earth is our home.

Let's think of ways that the Earth is our home. The Earth takes care of us in lots of ways. Who can name a way that the Earth provides for us? What does the Earth have that we need in order to live?

Answers would include:

Food: plants and animals.

Water: clean drinking water, washing, ice skating and swimming.

Trees: lumber for homes and paper. Leaves for shade and play. Fruit to eat.

Rocks: gravel for roads and stone for buildings.

Animals: horses and other animals to help us do our work, and dogs and cats to be our friends.

Air: clean air to breathe, breezes to keep us cool in the summer and fly our kites, cold winter winds to make us button up our coats. *(Accept and discuss answers.)*

These are several ways that the Earth takes care of us.

We need to take care of the Earth—just as it takes care of us.

Let's think of some ways that we can help take care of our home, the Earth. To help us get some ideas, let's first think of how we take care of the houses that we live in. Who can name a way that your family takes care of your house? What do you do when it gets dirty? Yes, you clean it up. When you have old newspapers, empty cereal boxes or old school papers, what do you do with them? You do not just throw this trash down on your floor, do you? You put it in the wastebasket or recycling bin. Are you careful with matches and candles around your house? Of course you are. You do not want your house to burn down. If you have a pet, do you feed it and make sure that it has a proper home?

The ways that we take care of our own homes are the same ways that we can help our Earth. We can pick up any trash that we see and throw it away. We can throw our trash in trash cans and not on the ground. We can be very careful with campfires and remind adults to completely put out their fires. We can help the Earth's animals by making sure they have food and protecting the places where they live.

By taking care of our world and the all things in it, we are remembering that our Earth is a very special place to live. We can remember this on Earth Day and all the other days of the year too.

Activities

1. Connect the dots, counting by twos. Read or tell the story of Earth Day and then let children connect the dots and color the picture.

2. Pick up trash. On your next trip to the playground, look for trash that needs to be picked up. Encourage children to pick up litter that they see in their neighborhood.

3. Discuss and draw the consequences. Why is it important to have clean air, water, and land? What would happen to our neighborhoods, streets, and highways if everyone threw their soda cans, dirty napkins, and hamburger wrappers out their car windows whenever they felt like it? The class can make a mural with two sides. On one side, they can draw their classroom, play-ground, neighborhood or park completely filled with all kinds of trash. On the other side, they can draw this same scene with no litter! Including a river or stream will help children learn that it is important to keep our waterways clean, too.

4. Learn about recycling. Make a list of everyday items that can be recycled such as glass, cans, paper, and plastic. Find out if the school recycles paper or other items. What happens to trash that is recycled? Draw a picture of the recycling symbol.

5. Make our Earth prettier. With an adult's help, plant flowers, trees, or other plants for birds, bees, and other insects to enjoy.

Earth Day

Name _____

CANS

From *Top Dot Tales*. Copyright © 2001 by Valerie Marsh (Alleyside Press)

The School Bus

Joseph was excited. Why? Because today was his first day at school. He was finally in Kindergarten. But he was nervous too. What if he couldn't find his room? What if the other kids didn't like him? What about the bus? Maybe you were concerned about some of these same things on your first day of school.

"Mom, I'm nervous about riding the bus" said Joseph.

"Honey, your big brother will take good care of you," said Mom.

Joseph's brother, Chris, said, "Yeah, Sport, we'll have fun riding the bus to school together. Gotta enjoy it this year 'cause next year I'm off to junior high. Say goodbye to Mom, Sport. We don't want her to be late." (His brother always called him "Sport," even though his name was really "Joseph.")

"But Mom, how much longer until the bus comes?" asked Joseph.

Mom answered, "It will be here in just a few minutes. I'll tell you what Joseph. You start singing the ABC song really slowly. Count how many times you can sing it before the bus gets here."

Joseph started singing the ABC song. Let's all sing it together.

(Hand out the school bus drawing on page 77 and crayons or pencils.) Now let's sing our ABC song again as we connect the alphabet letters on our paper. We will have to go really, really slowly because we want everyone to have time to find all the letters. *(Have children connect the letters on their paper, starting at the star.)*

What did you make? Yes, that's right. It is a bus!

Joseph sang his ABC song 15 times. Do you think you could sing the ABC song 15 times in a row? Would that make your big brother crazy? Maybe it would make *you* crazy! How do you think Joseph did on his first day of school? Yes, he had a wonderful first day at school, and everything turned out just fine.

Activities

1. Add details to the drawing. When everyone has finished their dot to dot drawing of the bus, ask the children what is missing on their bus. Have them draw the wheels. What else is missing? A stop sign? Encourage the children to draw their friends looking out of the windows of the bus. Then discuss the bus driver, and have the children draw their bus driver. Or, for fun, they could draw themselves as the driver or passengers of the bus.

2. Sing the "Wheels on the Bus" song, having the children adding their own verses.

3. Practice identifying the letters. Use a set of alphabet flash cards to sing the ABC song slowly enough that you can hold up each card as you and the children sing that letter. Review letters by presenting the letters in random order for the entire class or individual volunteers to identify.

4. Create a "congo line" bus by starting with one child (the driver), then adding kids as the bus stops to pick them up. Each new child holds on to the waist of the child in front of him. Make a circle around the room, then "arrive" at school.

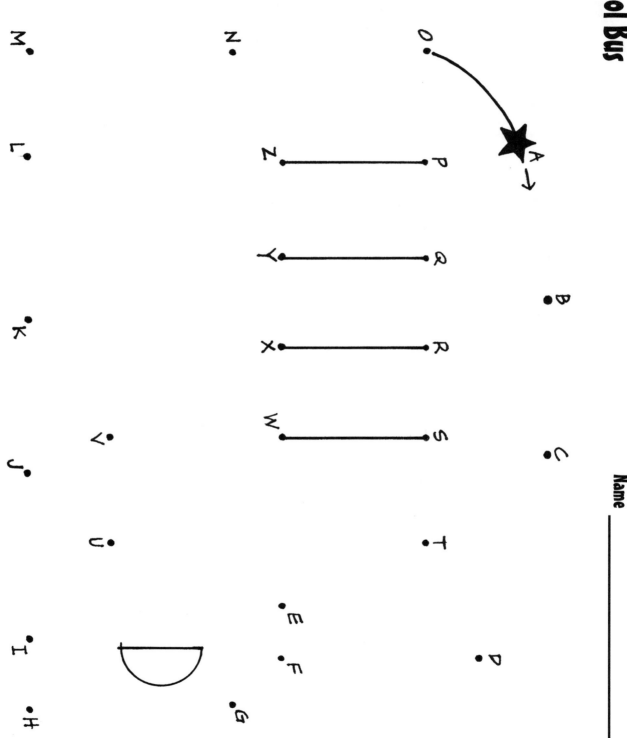

Name

From *Top Dot Tales.* Copyright © 2001 by Valerie Marsh (Alleyside Press)

Halloween

One day, two children got off the bus after a regular day at school. *(Pick two names of children in the class.)* Their school day was just the usual school day. But that evening was not going to be just the usual evening. It was going to be something special.

"I am so excited for tonight. I have my costume all ready to wear. Hey, Tom, let's find something special to help us celebrate," said Morgan.

Tom said, "Okay, where should we start?"

Morgan answered, "Let's start in the kitchen. I'm starving."

Tom and Morgan put their book bags down and went into the kitchen. They helped themselves to some cookies and milk.

Tom said, "Look, Morgan, I have the biggest cookie." *(Start at the star and connect the dots to draw a circle. What letter does this remind you of?)*

Morgan said, "Okay, okay, Tom. All the cookies are the same size."

Then Tom said, "But look Morgan, watch this." Tom nibbled all around the edge of his cookie. "Now, it's a little cookie. See, I have the smallest cookie," he said. *(Follow the dashes to draw a small circle inside the big circle. What letter does this remind you of?)*

Morgan said, "Okay, Tom, look at this. See this big piece of candy?" Morgan stuck a peppermint in her mouth. *(Starting at the square, connect the dots to make the other circle.)* A few moments later Morgan stuck out her tongue. The peppermint candy was stuck to the end of her tongue.

Tom said, "That's disgusting, Morgan."

Morgan answered, "No, Tom look. First it was a big piece of candy and now it is a little piece of candy." *(Follow the dashes to draw a small circle inside Morgan's big circle.)*

Tom yelled, "Hey, I know. Let's go out and get some apples from our tree to eat next."

Morgan answered, "Okay."

They picked some apples from the tree, took them inside, washed them off and ate them. *(Write the uppercase letter A between the two big circles that you drew. Why did we write the letter "A"? Yes, "A" is for apples.)*

Morgan said, "You know, we really need some milk to go with the rest of these cookies and these apples." She poured two glasses of milk, one for Tom, and one for herself. *(Trace each letter M. M is for milk.)*

Tom said, "Okay, Morgan, I just need one more thing to eat. Do we have any of those frozen waffles left?"

Morgan watched as Tom toasted some waffles, covered them in syrup and ate them. *(Trace a W for waffles under the letter A.)*

"Come on Tom. That is enough eating," Morgan said. "Mom will be home soon anyway to help us put on our make-up."

Tom and Morgan stepped out on the front porch and sat down on the front steps. A few minutes later, Mom pulled up in the driveway. She yelled out the car window, "I got you a surprise. Close your eyes and wait right there."

Mom lifted something out of the car and said, "Now open your eyes, and see my surprise."

Tom and Morgan looked at Mom's surprise. Tom yelled, "Alright! That is exactly what we need for tonight."

Do you know what Mom brought home for Tom and Morgan?

Yes, it was a pumpkin! *(Follow the dashed lines to draw a circle around all of your letters. What have you drawn? What was the holiday?)*

Activities

1. Discuss the story. Name the clues that let us know the holiday that Tom and Morgan looked forward to celebrating.

2. Make predictions. What do you think Morgan was going to wear for Halloween? What about Tom? What are you going to wear? Stress that Halloween is simply a special day to celebrate your imagination. By dressing up as different characters, we get to pretend to be a clown, astronaut, or fireman.

3. Learn opposites. There are some opposites in our story. Do you remember what an opposite is? Who can name two words that are opposite of each other? Remember Tom's cookie? First it was big and then he turned it into a small cookie. Give each of the children a cookie and encourage them to turn it into a small cookie.

4. Review letters and shapes. Discuss the shapes in the story. What shape is the cookie? What is the shape of a piece of candy? What shape do you see in the letter "A" and in the letters "M" and "W"?

Halloween

Name _____

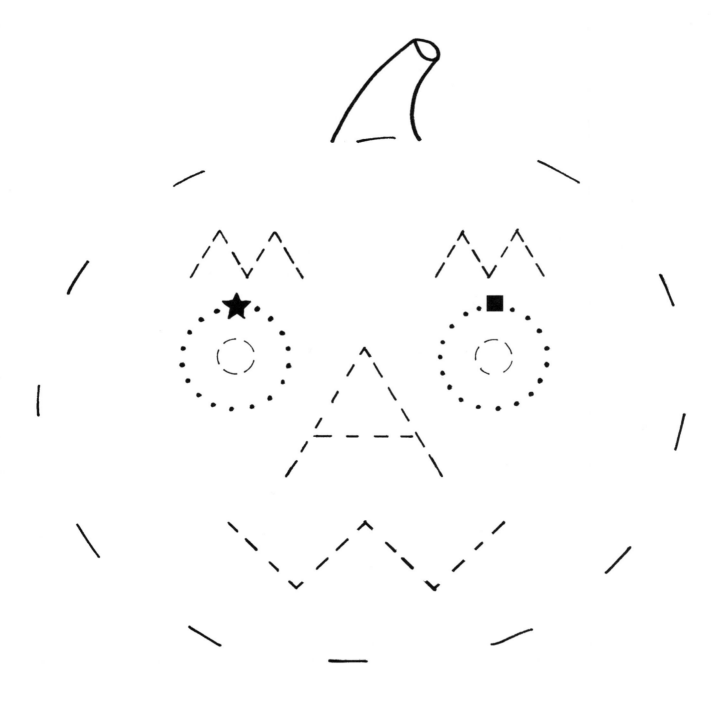

 From *Top Dot Tales*. Copyright © 2001 by Valerie Marsh (Alleyside Press)

An Alphabet Turkey

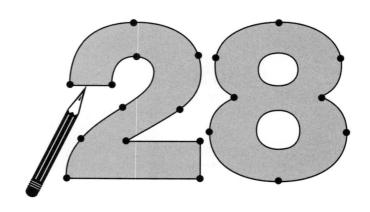

My family's turkey is

A wful

B ig,

and people

C ome to

D inner.

On Thanksgiving Day,

E verybody is

F amily.

After we eat, the visitors

G o

H ome.

I sit and

J ust

remember those turkey projects I

K ind of

L iked.

Why, I

M ade

N ine turkeys with globs of bright

O range

P aint.

One day we had a

Q uiet

R ecess. We kids made

S illy

T urkeys. We

U sed scraps of

V elvet and

W ire, then glued on

X -ray eyes.

And now my alphabet's done,

Y ou see.

I've talked Turkey A to

Z

Activities

1. Finish the turkey. After reading the poem, discuss beginning letters of the words in the poem so that they can discover that it makes an alphabet. Let children start at the star and make a circle by connecting up the uppercase letters. Then they should connect up lowercase letters. Last, they need to connect up each uppercase letter to its matching lowercase letter. Now the turkeys have feathers that the children can color!

2. Poem may also be copied. Let the children trace every letter, then, follow each letter as the poem is reread.

3. Make handprint turkeys.

   A. On a sheet of paper, trace each child's hand. Then they can color each finger to make more turkey feathers.

   B. Using a small brush and tempera paints, paint the palm of the child's hand brown and each finger and thumb a different color. Then carefully press the child's hand onto a piece of paper. When the colorful handprint is dry, the child may use a marker to color an eye, legs, a beak, and a waddle. This turkey handprint makes a nice holiday card. Using the other side of the paper, children may color a picture of themselves and their parent or another a special family member. Help them sign their name and make plans to give it to that family member.

4. Learn about traditions. Discuss the different ways that families celebrate the holiday of Thanksgiving. Let the children tell what they like about this holiday or how their families celebrate it. Ask the children to name their favorite foods.

5. Discuss the meaning of Thanksgiving. Discuss why people are thankful on this day. Ask the children what they are thankful. Encourage them to draw a picture to express their thanks.

Name _____

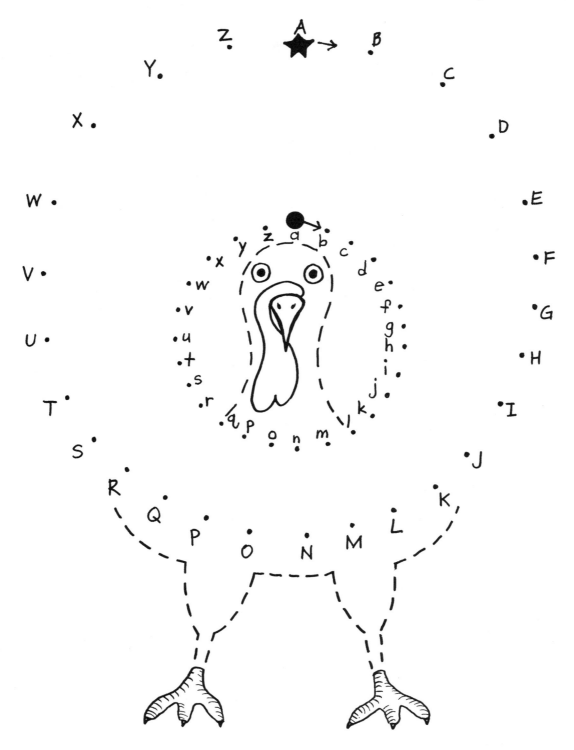

Happy Thanksgiving!

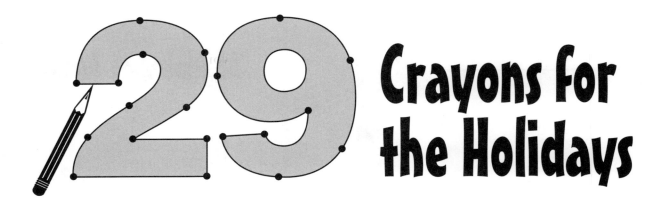

Crayons for the Holidays

Brendan was so excited because his favorite holiday _____ (*Christmas, Kwanzaa, Hanukkah*) was near. He loved everything about this holiday. He loved the special foods that his mom and grandfather made. He loved the candles and the lights. But most especially, he loved the gift giving. He always received lots of presents. But this year, Brendan decided to give everyone in his family a gift.

When Brendan looked in his piggy bank, he realized that he did not have very much money. How could he buy presents for everyone with what little money he had? Brendan put the coins in his pocket and walked into the kitchen. His mother was setting out their holiday candles. He always loved all their different colors. He looked at the candles and thought about all the people to whom he wanted to give presents. Then he got a perfectly wonderful idea.

Brendan said, "Mom, I need to go to the corner grocery store. I will be right back, okay?"

When Brendan returned, he was carrying a small package. His sister said, "Hey, Brendan, what's in your bag? Is it a present for me?"

Brendan answered, "Sort of." Then he went straight to his room and began work on his presents. First, he drew a picture of a red umbrella and wrote "To Mom" at the top of the paper. *(Start at the star and trace the numbers 1 to 10.)*

Next, Brendan drew a picture of a blue necklace and wrote his sister's name at the top. *(Now draw from 10 to 15.)*

Third, he drew a picture of a yellow flower and wrote "Grandma" at the top. *(Draw from 15 to 20.)*

Next Brendan colored a picture of a green scarf and wrote "Grandpa" on that picture. *(Draw from 20 to 25.)*

Orange was the next crayon that Brendan pulled out of his box. He colored a picture of a big bottle of orange soda pop and wrote "To Dad" on it. *(Draw from 25 to 30.)*

One the next piece of paper, Brendan wrote his brother's name and used his brown crayon to color a picture of a baseball glove. *(Draw from 30 to 35.)*

Black was the next crayon that Brendan pulled out of the crayon box. With this crayon, he made a picture of a dog collar. Do you know who this picture is for? *(Draw from 35 to 40.)*

Purple was the very last color and Brendan colored a big piece of purple bubble gum. This picture is for me. *(Draw from 40 to 45.)*

Now Brendan was all done with his pictures and he carefully put them all in a stack. Then he went back downstairs to the family room where everyone was getting ready to exchange presents.

Brendan was so excited about his pictures that he said, "I want to go first." He handed out his pictures to everyone and then said, "When I earn enough money, I will buy you this present. And until then, you can enjoy the picture that I made with my new box of......" What do you think Brendan bought at the grocery store? Yes, a box of crayons.

Activities

1. Finish the picture. Children may color the crayons the correct color.

2. Make a crayon rubbing. Place a piece of paper over an interesting surface, such as a leaf, bark, rough sandpaper, burlap. Using the side of a crayon, rub over the paper, capturing the texture of the surface.

3. Learn more about crayons. Find out about how crayons are made. How many are produced each year? When were they invented?

4. Make a bar graph. Ask each child to select a favorite color of crayon. Let each child color in one box on the bar graph to represent his color choice. Which color is the most popular?

Crayons for the Holidays

Name _____

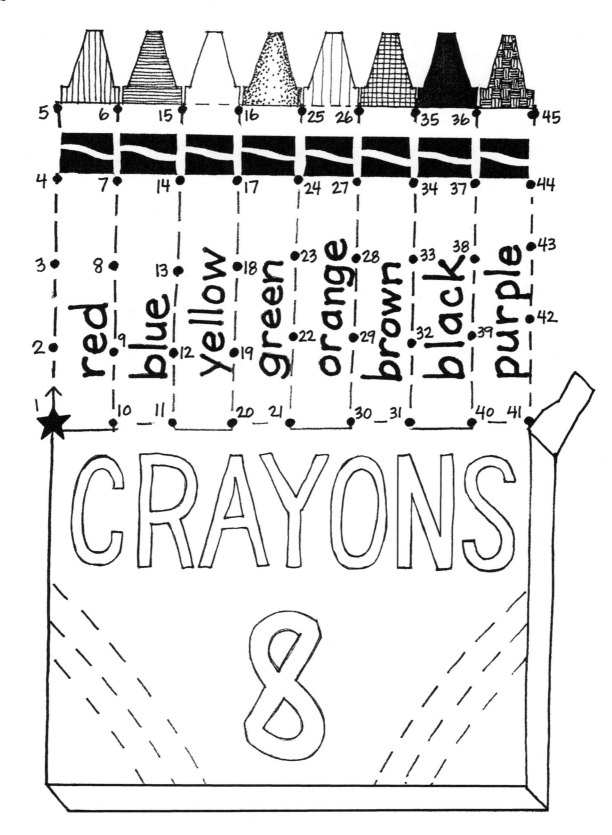

From *Top Dot Tales*. Copyright © 2001 by Valerie Marsh (Alleyside Press)

Fall Leaves

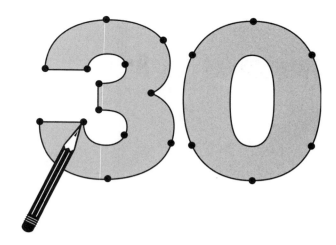

Swoosh, Swoosh!
The wind blows free!
It rattles every tree.
(Start at the star, draw from a to b to c.)

Whoosh, Whoosh!
The leaves fall down,
And scatter all around.
(Draw from c to d to e.)

Crunch, Crunch!
I walk on by
And kick at every leaf.
(Draw from e to f to g.)

Scrape, Scrape!
I use my rake
And pile them in a mound.
(Draw from g to h to i.)

Jump, Jump!
I leap and fly
Into the pile with glee!
(Draw from i to j to k.)

Up! Up!
I throw my leaves
They float back to the ground.

Activities

1. Act out the poem. They can sway like a tree in an imaginary wind. They can wiggle fingers for leaves falling down. They can walk in place, kicking imaginary leaves. They can "rake" leaves and jump up and down in their pile. While sitting down, they can throw their leaves up into the air.

2. Collect leaves. Encourage children to bring in pretty leaves that they find in their yard, on the playground, or at the bus stop. Ask the children to compare the leaf that they have drawn to several different leaves that their classmates have brought in.

3. Make leaves. Do leaf rubbings by placing a piece of paper over a leaf. Using the side of a crayon, rub back and forth across the paper.

4. Learn more about leaves. Identify different types of trees and leaves in nonfiction books. Help the children use the books to help name the leaves that they have collected.

5. Make your own dot-to-dot. Have the children make their own dot-to-dot leaf by tracing around a leaf and then adding their own dots and letters.

Fall Leaves

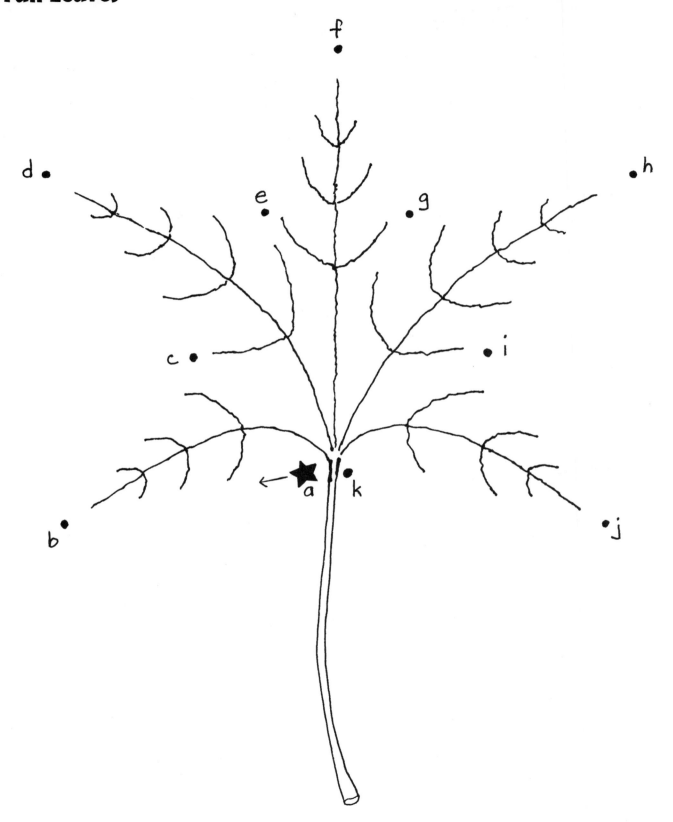

From *Top Dot Tales*. Copyright © 2001 by Valerie Marsh (Alleyside Press)

Winter Snowman

Sing to the tune of "Ten Little Indians."

1 little, **2** little, **3** little snowmen.
4 little, **5** little, **6** little snowmen.
7 little, **8** little, **9** little snowmen.
10 little snowman numbers.

"A" little, "B" little, "C" little snowmen.
"D" little, "E" little, "F" little snowmen.
"G" little, "H" little, "I" little snowmen.
All little snowman letters.

(If desired, continue the song using numbers 11–20 and the rest of the alphabet.)

Activities

1. Connect the dots. Encourage very young children to first use their fingers to trace the numbers and letters in order on their paper. Then after handing out crayons, sing the song slowly enough so that each child can trace the circles.

2. Color the snowman. Let children personalize the snowman by adding facial features, a hat, scarf, buttons, broom, and boots.

3. Make more snowmen. Children can make snowmen by gluing together large or small paper plates, coffee filters, or paper circles.

4. Have a snowball fight! Let each child make a "snowball" or two by wadding up an old piece of paper. Divide the class into two groups. Place a piece of masking tape on the floor to separate the room into two sections. On the count of three, children throw their snowballs over the line into the opposing team's court. Children pick up the snowballs as quickly as they can and throw them back over the line. When the teacher calls out "Stop!" the team with the fewest amount of snowballs on their side wins.

5. Cut out snowflakes using the designs on page 91. There are four designs to choose from, with varying levels of complexity. No matter which design you choose, photocopy it with the other three covered up. Then, have children fold along both lines and cut out the designs. Hang them around the room for an indoor snowfall!

Winter Snowman

Name _____

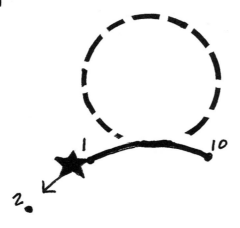

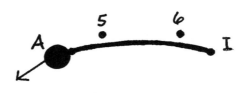

From *Top Dot Tales*. Copyright © 2001 by Valerie Marsh (Alleyside Press)

Snowflake Patterns

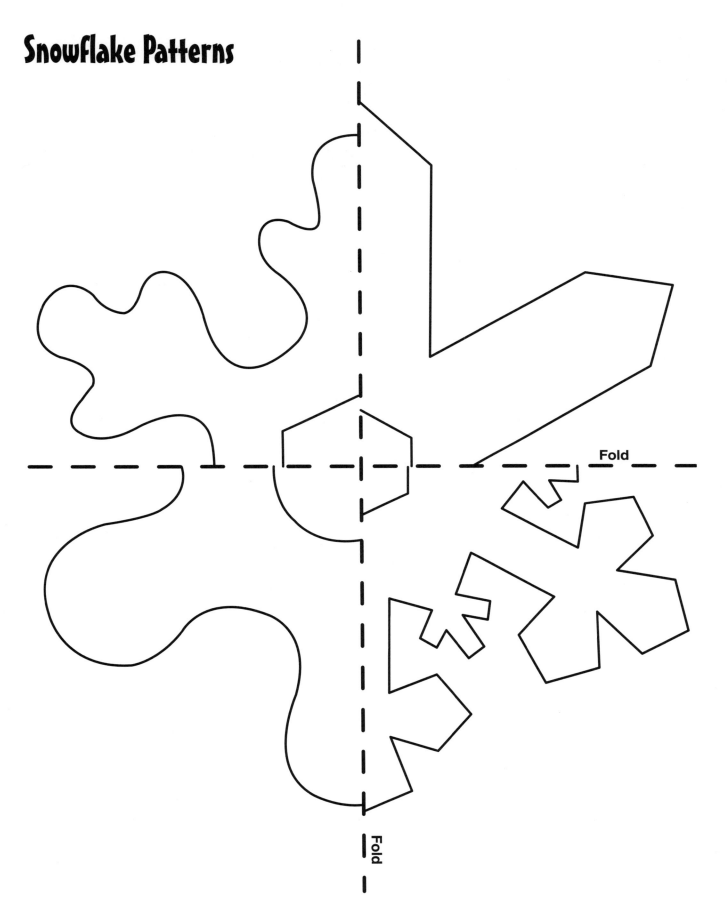

Fold

Fold

From *Top Dot Tales*. Copyright © 2001 by Valerie Marsh (Alleyside Press)

Spring Butterfly

Once there was a butterfly egg. *(**Start at the star, and connect A all the way around to G.**)* It was all alone on a leaf. Then one day it hatched. What do you think it did next? Yes, it started eating a hole in the leaf. As it ate the leaf, the little creature started to grow. *(**Draw a circle from H to M.**)* It ate another hole in the leaf and grew some more. *(**Draw a circle from N to S.**)* What did it become? That's right. It was a small caterpillar! Can you draw the antennae, some eyes, and a smiley face on your caterpillar?

Once there was a very little flower, called a "bud." *(**Draw from 1 to 5.**)* It had only one petal open. All the other flowers in the garden were all opened up. They thought that they were too big and too important to be friends with the little flower.

The little flower said, "I am lonely. I need a friend."

A small voice said, "I will be your friend."

Do you know who said that? Yes, it was the caterpillar.

The little flower said, "That would be great. I am small and you are small, so we can be small friends together."

The caterpillar said, "We will not always be small. We are both busy growing."

The caterpillar was right. Soon the little flower had opened another petal. *(**Draw from 6 to 10.**)*

A few days later the little flower had opened a third petal. *(**Draw from 11 to 15.**)* The little flower asked the caterpillar, "Are you okay, my friend?"

The caterpillar responded, "Yes, I am okay, but I am changing too."

The little flower opened yet another new petal. *(**Draw from 16 to 20.**)* Then little flower asked, "Are you there, little caterpillar? I don't see you."

Do you know where the caterpillar is? Yes, the caterpillar is not a caterpillar anymore. It is a beautiful butterfly. And it is right here. *(**Let children show their butterflies.**)*

Activities

1. Color the butterflies. Children may color their butterflies with markers, colored pencils or even paint.

2. Make more butterflies. Use coffee filters, markers and clothes pins. Let children color the coffee filters with felt tip markers. Then help them gently spray a *few* squirts of water on the coffee filter. The water will make the colors run together. When the filter is dry, gather it up in the middle, and secure it with a twist tie or a short length of pipe cleaner. Glue to clothespin. Put a piece of magnet tape on the other side of the clothespin and now it is a beautiful magnet.

3. Learn more about butterflies. Enjoy some nonfiction books together about butterflies.

4. Learn a butterfly's life sequence. Discuss the life cycle of a butterfly, using the sequencing words of first, second, third, and last.

Spring Butterfly

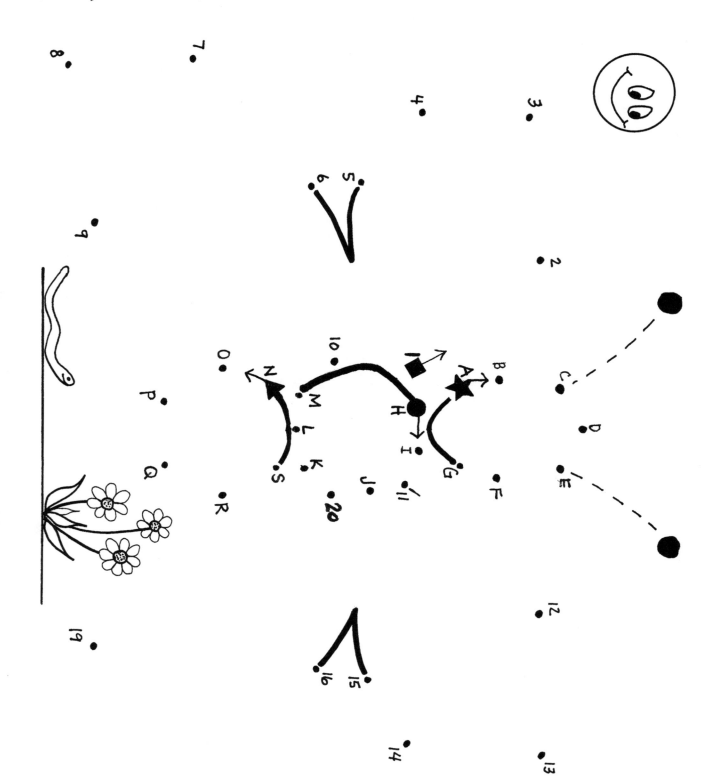

From *Top Dot Tales.* Copyright © 2001 by Valerie Marsh (Alleyside Press)

Summer Sailboat

Lance loved to play with sticks. *(Draw a line from the little triangle to the big triangle.)* In the spring, he drew in the sand box with a stick. In the summer, he liked drawing his initials in the mud with a stick. *(Connect the dots from 1 to 2 to 3. This makes the letter "L." "L" is for Lance.)*

In the fall, he whacked fallen leaves into the air with a stick. Yes, just thinking about sticks made Lance smile. *(Connect all the little squares into a smile.)*

Sometimes it rained and Lance could not go out to play. If it was not lightning, his mother would let Lance go out to splash in the puddles in front of his house. *(Connect small circles. This makes a puddle.)* What did Lance need so he would not get wet? *(Accept all answers.)*

Yes, he needed an umbrella. Where was his umbrella? *(Turn your paper around so it is upside-down.)* Yes, it is right here.

But do you know what made Lance smile even more than walking in the rain or playing with a stick? *(Turn paper back around.)* Yes, he smiled from ear to ear when he took a ride with Grandpa in his Grandpa's sailboat. *(Draw A to B to C and back to A. What shape did you make? Yes, it is a triangle.)* Where is Grandpa's sailboat? Why, it is right here! *(Look at your sailboat.)*

Activities

1. Review the story. Discuss with the children how each piece of the drawing comes together to make a sailboat. For example, the two smiles make the boat, and the letter L becomes part of the triangle to make the sail, doesn't it?

2. Review the shapes. Ask the children to trace over the triangles with their finger, and find the squares and circles.

3. Add to the drawing. Children can draw Lance and his Grandfather in the boat.

4. Learn more shapes. Let children draw the basic shapes of circle, square, triangle, rectangle, and oval. Name some of these basic shapes that they can see in the classroom. What shape is the clock? What shape is the table? Perhaps they can think of other things to draw, using these basic shapes.

Summer Sailboat

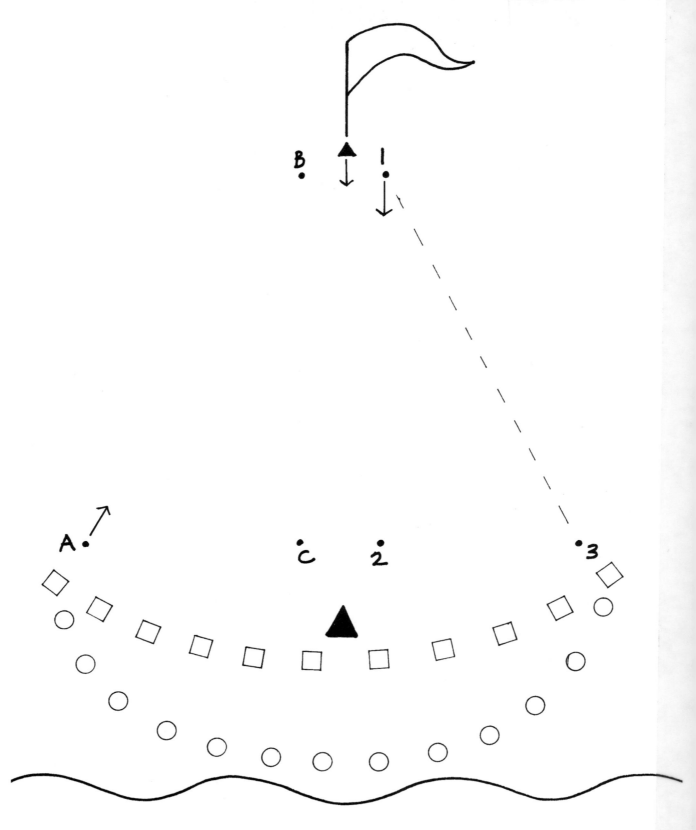

From *Top Dot Tales*. Copyright © 2001 by Valerie Marsh (Alleyside Press)